DOR PILGRIMAGES

A MILLENNIUM HANDBOOK

PETER KNIGHT and MIKE POWER

Publishers note
Whilst every care has been taken to ensure that all the information contained in this
book is correct neither the authors or publishers can accept any responsibility for any
inaccuracies that might occur

ISBN 1898073 21 X

Ist published August 2000

Front cover:
Photographs: Peter Knight & Mike Power
Layout: Graham Whiteman.

CONTENTS

ACKNOWLEDGMENTS

The authors would like to thank the following for helping us with this book:

Dr Michael Eckhard of Hamburg Museum, for permission to use Frido Witte's woodcut; Simon and Schuster, for permission to quote from M Scott Peck's 'In Search of Stones'; Joy Swan, for the photo of Alderley Edge; Terence Meaden for the photo of the stone head at Nine Stones; Andrew Lane, for bringing to our attention the stone at Melbury Osmund and the photograph of it and the ley details associated with Wynford Eagle; Jenny and Jack Cummings and Alan Gibbons, for walking three of the pilgrimages, offering valuable information and insights; Yana Nilsson and Gary Biltcliffe, for information on Dorset's sacred wells; Pauline Stanley for spotting the Green man at Child Okeford; Gill Coombes for accompanying Mike Power at times and for reading the manuscript. Finally a thank you to all those people, known and unknown, who assisted the authors during our research and pilgrimage walking.

One
MILLENNIUM PILGRIMAGES – WHY NOW?

Pilgrimage – *a journey to a shrine or other sacred place.*
Collins English Dictionary, 2nd Edition.

Judging by the very definition of 'pilgrimage' above you may have already been a pilgrim without realising it. Thousands journey across Dorset every year visiting sites of spiritual and religious interest. This practice is, of course, repeated by millions across the world.

Countless travellers journey to ancient sites, shrines, holy wells and other localities which have a feel of the 'sacred' about them. Many of these latter-day wayfarers may not, in fact, be able to define why they are drawn to such places. However, others may describe some inner voice calling them or that the very destination itself, the sacred site, beckons them.

The essence of pilgrimage is that it is a journey TO not FROM. It is not an escape, it is a quest. A pilgrimage can be viewed as a metaphor for our whole life. Psychiatrist and author M Scott Peck concludes (in *'In Search of Stones'*) "….life is a pilgrimage, or rather can be if we use it as such. The notion that human existence can be a pilgrimage is as ancient as the written word". He goes on to state that the act of pilgrimage is a part of our psyche and of the collective psyche of our species.

In undertaking rambling, hill-walking and long distance trekking, perhaps the participant is seeking out, on some level, their distant roots, walking in the footsteps of our ancestors, both literally and metaphorically. Going back in time, so to speak, helps connect us to the present in a more fulfilling way.

The spirit of the wayfarer on the open road is captured in this old German woodcut, by Frido Witte (used with permission)

"Ancient Pilgrim Approaches The Stones," by Peter Knight

The dawning of the new millennium marks a pivotal point in the recreational and spiritual freedoms of our culture. We have more free time on our hands nowadays to pursue activities that nourish the mind, body and spirit. Walking continues to grow into an immensely popular pastime. The success of Mike Power's "Pub Walks" series is ample evidence of this trend. The popularity of Peter Knight's two guides to Dorset's ancient heritage likewise bears testament to the flourishing growth in the number of people yearning to connect with the spiritual essence of the land and its sacred sites. A combination of both subjects would seem to

be a very appropriate synthesis for the millennial passage.

Dorset is blessed with a wealth of unspoilt countryside, criss-crossed by a web of public footpaths and bridleways. It is home to an exceptional number of prehistoric, Roman, early Christian and, indeed, natural sacred places. These range from stone circles to ancient crosses, from holy wells to Roman temples, from countless barrows to dozens of old atmospheric, isolated chapels. These are the relics of profuse spiritualities spanning some 6000 years.

We have compiled in this book an offering of 10 newly-envisaged pilgrimages, designed with a sacred site (be it pre-Christian, Christian or natural) as their destination. Yet they are more than this, encompassing – (a) a sacred site as their starting point, enabling not only an immediate immersion into the sanctity of the journey, but also facilitating each pilgrimage to be walked in a reverse direction; (b) several sacred sites en route, allowing rest, shelter, further interest, encouragement and reinstatement of the journey's intent and (c) passage through beautiful, uplifting and tranquil scenery, enabling close interaction with the landscape and the Spirit therein.

All three elements come together on each pilgrimage to hopefully promote a feeling of well-being, both inner and outer, in the modern pilgrim. For the magic in not merely seeking new landscapes without, but the quest for new landscapes within. True, a pilgrimage of the foot-slogging kind can be the trigger for experiencing outer calm and contacting the true face of Nature. But, more than that, it can ultimately aid one's search for inner serenity and exposing our own nature. This guide will, it is hoped, be a conduit for such a noble quest.

All ten pilgrimages, personally walked during 1999, range from 11 – 14 miles, are described in detail and accompanied by photographs and a comprehensive sketch map. Every 'stop' of interest was visited, enabling us to pass on interesting information, personal experiences, access restrictions and such like. It was felt that although Dorset still retains vestiges of ancient pilgrimage ways, a new millennium demands new pilgrimage routes – fresh starts new beginnings. Yet despite this some of our walks do follow, for part of their course, ancient ridgeway tracks, old footpaths and sunken green roads, all with their own character. We also include some pilgrimage sites of old, such as chapels, stone crosses, holy wells and other shrines, not to mention stone circles and the like. Such places are timeless and sacred by any definition, making them worthy havens for today's wayfarer.

The new pilgrim, you no less, will follow the new routes, yet aspire to connect with the old. The ancient act and benefits of pilgrimage, still carried out by millions across the world today, will conceivably be rekindled. In making a pilgrimage we partake in something that is characteristically and profoundly human. Perhaps we are not 'going out there', but really 'coming home'.

This project has certainly been a meaningful and positive undertaking for the authors. It heralds our commitment to preserving our ancient paths, public rights of way, sacred sites and the breathtaking countryside that is Dorset. We hope the millennial pilgrim will gain as much from walking the pilgrimages as we did devising them.

⟡⟡⟡⟡⟡⟡⟡⟡⟡⟡⟡⟡⟡⟡⟡⟡⟡⟡⟡⟡⟡⟡⟡

"O, how I long to travel back
And tread again that ancient track"
(From *'The Retreate'* Henry Vaughan, 17th C.)

⟡⟡⟡⟡⟡⟡⟡⟡⟡⟡⟡⟡⟡⟡⟡⟡⟡⟡⟡⟡⟡⟡⟡

TWO
PILGRIMAGE - A WALK ON THE WILD SIDE

"We walk by faith and not by sight"
St. Paul.

IN THE FOOTSTEPS OF OUR ANCESTORS

Because of the universal belief in inherently sacred places, many localities have been and remain magnets for pilgrims of all religious and spiritual persuasions, although the act of journeying from one's homeland to a far flung shrine or other venerated place goes back to antiquity. The ancient Greeks would make long treks from the corners of their empire to hear the oracle speak at Delphi. It is recorded that every September a 14-mile procession took place from Athens to the temple complex at Eleusis, sacred to the god of healing, Asklepios. The Roman Pliny records that a man named Sansnos wrote on

A spring equinox ceremony by Druids at Avebury. Ancient sites have been the focus of similar rituals for centuries

an Egyptian wall the maxim "Revere the Divine. Sacrifice to all the gods. Travel in homage to each temple...."

Nearer to home there is little doubt that major Neolithic and Bronze Age temples, such as Stonehenge and Avebury, were the destination of prehistoric pilgrims. The subject of ley lines often sparks controversial debate, but it seems increasingly likely that many of them developed into track ways that would have been used to visit sacred sites en route. Alfred Watkins, the discoverer of ley lines in the 1920s, quotes from old texts, many of them Biblical, to support a more spiritual link to leys, such as *"Make straight paths for your feet".* (Hebrews, xii, 13). In 1678, in fact, John Bunyan wrote in his 'Pilgrims Progress' *"Look before thee, dost thou see the narrow way, it is straight as a rule can make it. This is the way thou must go."*

Perhaps these metaphors have ancient origins, dating back, may be, to leys. In addition to those tracks which may have originally evolved from leys, many ancient ridgeway routes link prehistoric spiritual sites. These would have been used not just for trade purposes, but also for those attending important festival ceremonies.

The Celts gathered at sacred places where they believed that gods or goddesses were in residence, and could be approached. In Celtic legend the fairy king Gwynn ap Nudd was thought to hold court within Glastonbury Tor. The hot springs at Bath were the home of the goddess Sulis and was a pilgrim destination long before the Romans arrived there. The Celts saw pilgrimage journeys as metaphors for the heroic tales of the Quest, and sought to emulate the adventure of their gods and goddesses, heroes and heroines.

The 14th Century theologian, Ibn Battula (the 'Traveller of Islam', as he became known) spoke of the impulse to visit scared places:

"I set out alone finding no companion to cheer the way with friendly intercourse, swayed by an overmastering impulse within me, a long cherished desire to visit those glorious sanctuaries."

Modern day Australian Aborigines travel to sites sacred to them and their ancestors, and journey on foot for many miles and days along well trodden 'song lines'. During these Dreamtime walkabouts to ancestral sacred sites they venerate large boulders, caves, burial mounds and even significant trees.

❖❖❖❖❖❖❖❖❖❖❖❖❖❖❖❖❖❖❖❖❖❖

*"Many roads thou has fashioned,
All of them lead to the Light."*
(Kipling, "Song to Mithras the Sun God")

❖❖❖❖❖❖❖❖❖❖❖❖❖❖❖❖❖❖❖❖❖❖

THE LONG AND WINDING ROAD

In Dorset major prehistoric centres, such as Knowlton (Pilgrimage 9), Mount Pleasant Henge and Maumbury were the scenes of ceremonies and gatherings at key times of the turning year, such as Winter Solstice, Beltaine, Samhain, Summer Solstice and so on. One can envisage streams of travellers descending on such places to witness sacred rites. Even smaller sites, such as lonely stone circles and solitary megaliths, would have been revered and today still pull on our spiritual roots. M. Scott Peck concludes (in 'In Search of Stones'), *"In searching for stones, we are searching for something that might be holy, a place where we can feel in the presence of holiness....."*

The journey to these places during prehistoric times and even into the Roman occupation, would often be treacherous with few proper tracks to guide the traveller. The situation in Dorset had only marginally improved by medieval times, when Christian pilgrimage routes began to appear. For this reason crosses were erected in large numbers across the countryside to guide pilgrims along their way. Very often prehistoric megaliths were re-fashioned for the purpose, such as at Minterne Parva (near Cerne Abbas) and at Tarrant Crawford (Pilgrimage 9). Alfred Pope (in 'Old Stone Crosses of Dorset') saw them as providing *"...excitement to holy feelings before reaching these places of worship."* Richer travellers would leave alms for poorer wayfarers who might follow them.

Pope noted that these pilgrimage/ wayside crosses often follow well-defined pilgrimage routes. For instance, there is a line of old stone crosses (and sites of former ones now lost) up the Stour Valley from Wimborne Minster to Shaftesbury Abbey and another between Milton Abbey and Shaftesbury. They mark, adds Pope,not only medieval pilgrimage itineraries but also circuits used by preaching friars who went forth ministering their faith.

Langton Herring stone cross (close to Pilgrimage 5) lies midway between the port of Weymouth and Abbotsbury with its abbey site and chapel (Pilgrimage 3). Pope surmises that the ancient cross/megalith at Minterne Parva (AS* Page 172) would have been passed by pilgrims travelling from Sherborne and Shaftesbury to Cerne Abbey and vice versa. Jackman's Cross (Pilgrimage 4) is situated high on the ridgeway at Grimstone Down. It too may have been a stop by pilgrims wayfaring between Cerne, Shaftesbury and Abbotsbury. The stone cross at Sydling St Nicholas (AS p.175 and SD p.257) may have likewise marked routes between these abbeys. Almost forgotten in the garden of Cornhill

Cottage, West Melbury (Pilgrimage 8) is another medieval cross base. It once stood at the nearby crossroads and marked a pilgrimage from south Dorset north to Shaftesbury Abbey.

THE WELL TRODDEN PATH

❖-❖

'The pilgrimage is like an ever flowing river.'
(Ayatolla Al-Udhma Khaminei, Hajj, 1996)

❖-❖

Sacred and holy wells, springs and rivers have long since been major pilgrimage destinations, right back to prehistoric/classical times. Water is the elixir of Life, the gift of God, the waters of the Goddess, depending on culture and beliefs. In India the Gangees attracts millions of devotees every year to bathe in its sacred waters. Indian

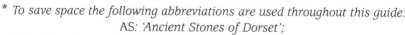

* To save space the following abbreviations are used throughout this guide:
AS: *'Ancient Stones of Dorset';*
SD: *'Sacred Dorset- On the Path of the Dragon'. Both by Peter Knight.*

scholar, A.Bharati, quotes an old woman speaking of her devotion: "...so we walk towards the source of the Gangees, and if we die in the effort that is the most desirable death we can meet."

In Britain, thousands of latter day pilgrims visit holy/curative wells and springs, many of which date back to the dawn of Christianity and beyond. The Chalice Well at Glastonbury, Madron Well in Cornwall and Walsingham in Kent attract legions of visitors annually to partake of the, reputably, curative waters.

In Dorset wells and springs, many of some antiquity, continue to be focal points for travellers today (These are dealt with in depth in SD* p.98-119). Many of these provided refreshment to the medieval pilgrim en route to religious foundations, but some are, in fact, worthy of being pilgrimage destinations in their own right. The Silver or Augustine's Well at Cerne Abbas is such a place. It nestles in an atmospheric corner of ruined abbey grounds (Pilgrimage 4). Lady's Well at Hermitage (Pilgrimage 2) is situated between Sherborne and Cerne Abbas. Betwixt the Abbeys of Abbotsbury and Bindon was the former well at Warmwell. Pilgrims to Christchurch Priory were invited to partake (after purchasing!) the waters of Tutton's Well nearby, said to be a cure for eye complaints.

Several springs and wells are included in this guide offering the new pilgrim both physical and spiritual nourishment.

Upwey Wishing well, c.1880.

MIRACLES? WALK THIS WAY....

❖❖❖❖❖❖❖❖❖❖❖❖❖❖❖❖❖❖❖❖❖❖❖

*"The pilgrimage goes beyond necessity
and utility into the purely human realms
of imagination and spirit."*

(Derek Brewer 'Chaucer and His World')

❖❖❖❖❖❖❖❖❖❖❖❖❖❖❖❖❖❖❖❖❖❖❖

The shrine of St Edward the Martyr, Shaftesbury Abbey.

Countless pilgrimage destinations across the world are the localities of reported manifestations of miracles and apparition. Lourdes in France (scene of a vision of the Virgin Mary in 1858) and Guadeloupe in Spain (statue of Virgin Mary phenomena) are two classic examples of places developing into major pilgrimage foci from humble beginnings. Britain too has a copious number of "miracle sites" and Dorset in no exception. Four places and their folklore deserve closer inspection, two of which are pilgrimage destinations in this guide.

The shrine of St Edward the Martyr, son of Edgar the Peaceable, stands in the grounds of Shaftesbury Abbey (Pilgrimage 8). In 987 he was murdered by his stepmother and the body thrown either into a river or well, depending on the folklore. Later a pillar of light illuminated the spot and a blind woman was healed. Her cottage was, in turn, burnt to the ground but the following morning she saw water trickling from the ashes which developed into a spring which bore witness to further miracles.

In 1001 the body was moved to the shrine at Shaftesbury, white broom springing up miraculously along the funeral route. Eventually the body was removed from the shrine and at the opening of the tomb it·is reported that a sweet odour was emitted. The shrine and the tales of miracles helped to make the Abbey very wealthy. The streets of Shaftesbury thronged with pilgrims for some decades.

Inside the church at Whitchurch Canonicorum stands the shrine of St Wite or Candida. The bones of a small woman were found in 1900 in a casket. The 13th-century shrine has three large holes where the sick and diseased would place their limbs whilst praying to the saint for a restoration of their health. St Wite is a very obscure figure, but it has been speculated that she was a saint from Brittany. St Wite's Well at nearby Morecombelake (see SD p.112-115) has folklore that its waters cure eye complaints. Both the shrine and the well became pilgrimage destinations. Nigel Pennick (see Bibliography) gives evidence that St Wite was merely the Christianisation of the Celtic triple-breasted goddess Gwen Teirbron. This may account for the shrine having three healing holes.

"Give me my scallop-shell of quiet,
My staff of faith to walk upon,
My gown of glory, hope's true gauge,
And thus I'll take my pilgrimage"
Sir Walter Raleigh

The Cross and Hand Stone stands in solitude high on Batcombe Down (Pilgrimage 4 and AS page164). Estimates for its date range from prehistoric to medieval but according to legend it was erected to mark the spot of a miraculous event. According to folklore a medieval village priest was on his way to administer the last rites to a dying shepherd. En route he lost his pyx, a sacred silver casket. He set out to retrace his steps, walking back in foul weather. He then saw a beam of light coming through the otherwise rainy skies and at the foot of it lay the lost pyx. All around stood animals, wild and domesticated. Retrieving the holy object he then proceeded to the dying man to give him the viaticum. The following morn he returned to the locality of the miracle and vowed to erect a monument to it.

This tale is typical of many across the world and has in fact parallels with other sites of prehistoric age that later became Christianised. It made political sense to endow existing (pagan) sacred sites with more saintly Christian miracles and 'acts of God'.

The next tale does at least tie in with historical events. Above Milton Abbey, nestling in the woods on the hill is St Catherine's Chapel (Pilgrimage 7 destination). King

The shrine of St Wite, Whitchurch Canonicorum. Note the holes for the insertion of diseased limbs.

The Holy Thorn and the Tor at Glastonbury, a place sacred to many religions and cults.

Athelstan and his army were camped on the hill before going into battle with the invading Danes. Apparently two miracles took place that night. Whilst Athelstan slept he had a vision of victory over his enemies. Later that same night a Danish raiding party attacked seeking to kill the King. He leapt up at the sound of the commotion and raced out to fight, but feeling for his sword he realised his scabbard was empty and he was unarmed. Apparently he went to the crest of the hill and prayed to God and miraculously his sword returned to its scabbard. The Danes were put to flight and victory was assured.

So moved was Athelstan by these two divine interventions that he founded the abbey in 934. Similar stories of miracles are found across Dorset, such as the beam at Christchurch Priory and Augustine's miraculous striking of the ground with his staff to release the waters of the spring at Cerne. Some of these tales were flagrant inventions by local monks and priests whilst others were perhaps the corruption of existing folklore to Christianise pagan sacred sites. Whatever the case, such places are enshrined with mystery and some have become pilgrimage destinations of the faithful and the pious.

Many pilgrimage routes and their destinations across the world transcend religious boundaries, being sacred to more than a single belief system. For instance, Adam's Peak in Sri Lanka is sacred to Buddhists, Taoists, Muslims and Christians alike. Glastonbury is likewise a spiritual centre for many orthodox and 'alternative' spiritual groups. Jerusalem is another classic example of a centre of multi-cultural religious devotion. St Michael's Mount, on the Cornish coast, first became associated with St Michael in AD 495 and is a major Christian pilgrimage focus today. Yet it is of considerable importance to pagans and Druids, who will tell you it lies near one end of the famous Michael ley line. This alignment passes through prehistoric and Christian localities, such as Avebury and Glastonbury. The ley aligns with the May Day (Beltaine) sunrise, a fertility festival of ancient origin. There is a blend of prehistoric, Christian and natural sites and it is this synthesis that we have striven to achieve in this guide.

Eade and Sallnow (in 'Contesting the Sacred: The Anthology of Christian Pilgrimage') analyse these multi-religious phenomena. They state "What confers upon a major shrine its essential universal character is its capacity to absorb and reflect a multiplicity of religious discourses, to be able to offer a variety of clients what each of them desires". It has been said of sacred sites that it is the LOCALITY that is sacred, not just what has occurred or been built there. When we visit such a place we also connect with those who have gone before us and we partake in experiences others may have had. In 'No Destination' Satish Kumar observed "I was in the company of those who had preceded me". And, in turn, people will walk in our footsteps too.

✤✤✤✤✤✤✤✤✤✤✤✤✤✤✤✤✤✤✤✤✤✤✤

"There's no discouragement,
Shall make him once relent,
His first avowed intent,
To be a pilgrim."

(John Bunyan hymn 'Who would True Valour See')

✤✤✤✤✤✤✤✤✤✤✤✤✤✤✤✤✤✤✤✤✤✤✤

THREE

WALKING AS MEDITATION - SAUNTERING FOR THE SOUL

"...footpaths often induce that comtemplative state which is the soil for visionary experience." Kim Taplin, 'The English Path'

Ramblers and long distance trekkers will tell you that the very act of walking is uplifting. A trek through isolated countryside can become, quite literally, a walking meditation. The automatic act of steady rhythmic walking (as opposed to a galloping dash) can release the mind to both experience and express. Taken to its ultimate, one can enter some altered state of awareness, a realm of deeper perceptions.

U.S. naturalist John Muir (1838-1914) experienced this connection between walking and contemplation; *"I only went out for a walk and finally concluded to stay out until sundown, for going out, I found, was really going in."* Modern Indian pilgrim and scholar Satish Kumar concluded (in 'No Destination') that *"Walking in itself was an end, a form of meditation, a way of being."* This is echoed by Trappist monk Thomas Merton (1915-68) who metaphorically observed *"Our real journey in life is interior".* *"Walking along country roads",* mystic author G W Russell noted, *"my senses were expectant of some unveiling about to take place."*

Long distance walking as a positive activity in its own right is still under-valued. Alterations of the thought and emotional processes occur. The rhythmic action that walking entails can ignite daydreams, release flashes of insight, timeless mystical moments. The week or month-long Dreamtime 'walkabouts' of the Aborigines reflect this. They journey across the land yet see and sense it with their inner selves.

"I went out in search of Shiva, the omnipresent Lord.
Having wandered, I found him in my own body."
14th century Kashmiri mystic woman

The experience of a walking pilgrimage involves movement across time and space, yet it is more than this. It calls for a response by pilgrims to what they encounter along the way and at their arrival at the destination. A two-way dialogue can be opened up between the participant and the landscape and its sacred sites. A pilgrimage walk, if experienced to the extreme, can be the release not only for rushes of adrenaline, but also for inner changes and bursts of perception. This is due, not in small part, to the pilgrim being in a strange land, walking to unknown places and at a pace staggeringly slow compared to their normal everyday dash and jostle. By increasing the speed of travel through the land we certainly seem to lose our closeness to it. The unique combination of rhythmic walking and the period of relative isolation heightens and sharpens our normally deadened senses. In *'Celtic Sacred Landscapes'*, Nigel Pennick concurs: *"In contrast with the random scenes glimpsed fleetingly by the motorist, those who walk experience authentic contact with the places through which they pass."*

Perhaps whilst pilgrimage walking we could do well to follow our intuition when it whispers to us. If a tree calls you go over to it, sit under or against it, hug it, whatever *feels* right. If you suddenly have an urge to peer though a gap in the hedgerow GO FOR IT. It may lead you to the most uplifting and meaningful moments of the whole journey! Many Buddhists walk in total silence, to attune themselves to the land and themselves. The 'Sound of Silence' of Nature can be deafening. In silence you can hear the inner workings of both mind and landscape. If walking a pilgrimage with one or more companions, do not feel obliged to engage in conversation. You could, in fact, designate yourselves period of muteness. Such silences will facilitate the perception of the subtle sounds and language of both Nature and yourself.

Many people approach a sacred site, such as a stone circle, with a final dash and make a race for it, a bit like a sprinter reaching for the line! Agreed, there can be a rush of excitement as one approaches a sacred destination and this is part of the whole experience. But it is a more beneficial approach to perhaps stop, be still, listen, sense and SLOW DOWN both mind and body before entering. Humility and silence are valuable assets to understanding, appreciating and above all EXPERIENCING sacred places. Do not forget that you are invading the locality, bringing with you noise, movement and even unwanted energies. A humble, respectful attitude is important in unravelling the true essence and sanctity of sacred sites.

In his excellent 'Re-visioning the Earth', Paul Devereux notes that a pilgrimage can take the participant *"out of routine levels of consciousness to conditions that expose the mind to the possibility of sensibilities beyond the pale of civilised life…"*. Perhaps the reader can learn to walk slowly, to walk with all the senses wide open and receptive to all experiences encountered. Sauntering, indeed, for the soul.

A 19th C photograph of Buddhist pilgrims climbing Mount Fuji in silent procession.

✦✧✦✧✦✧✦✧✦✧✦✧✦✧✦✧✦✧✦✧✦✧✦✧✦✧✦

*"Thus saith the Lord, Stand ye in the
ways, and see and ask for the old paths,
where is the good way and walk therein,
and ye shall find rest for your souls."*
The Bible, Jeremiah, vi,16.

✦✧✦✧✦✧✦✧✦✧✦✧✦✧✦✧✦✧✦✧✦✧✦✧✦✧✦

This road sign symbolises our individual urge to push beyond the known, to push towards 'the edge'. (photo by Joy Swan)

FOUR

SACRED LANDSCAPES - WALKING ON MOTHER

"In beauty, I walk to the direction of the rising sun,
In beauty, I walk to the direction travelling with the sun,
In beauty, I walk to the direction of the setting sun,
In beauty, I walk, all around me the land is beauty,
In beauty, I walk." American Navajo chant

The view of tribal and aboriginal cultures of today (and probably that of our ancestors too) is that the land is a living, mythological landscape on to which legends are inscribed. The earth is viewed with the soul rather than the level of the body. Travelling a pilgrimage across such a perceived land can transform the journey into a 'magical mystery tour' indeed. The old adage that it is the journey not the destination that is important is certainly true of pilgrimage. This is heightened to new levels with the realisation that the earth, the very land on which we tread, is sacred unto itself.

Hindus, Buddhists, Pagans, Druids and tribal societies recognise the sanctity of NATURAL sacred places. Very often ancient sites, shrines and temples were positioned with the surrounding landscape in mind – THE SITES BECAME PART OF THAT LANDSCAPE, not just structures built on it. Many such sites will be encountered in this guide, demonstrating the close spiritual connection of Man and the land in ages past.

Long distance walking can open up a two-way communication between the walker and Nature, between the inner realms of humans and the very spirit of the land. It was Lebanese poet and mystic Kahlil Gibran who observed *"And forget not that the earth delights to feel your bare feet and the wind longs to play with your hair"*. Ralph Waldo Emerson concluded that *"Nature is the immense shadow of Man"*, suggesting that

Nature is our mirror and that we are inexplicably and umbilically linked to it.

In partaking of solitary walking in isolated countryside one may slip effortlessly into an altered state of awareness. This results from the combination of one's faith and beliefs with the very energies and atmosphere of the landscape and its sacred sites. We need to open up the landscape with all our senses, to smell, taste, feel, hear, touch, intuit and SEE the land. Walking with humility and respect for the body on which we tread is the basis of many cultures, both present and past. The Aborigines and American Indians of today (at least until recent times) went barefoot or with moccasins, so as to feel every grain they walked upon. This is equivalent to the respect shown by removal of footwear by Hindus, Buddhists and Muslims entering their holy places.

Pilgrimage is a physical act that takes people into the largely unknown realms of Nature. Pilgrim and scholar Rana Singh stated that pilgrimage is *"...the human quest for a divine connection between Man and environment"*. Indeed we enter the twilight world of Merlin, fairy tales and the mystic. Many have experienced this secret side of Nature.

Shakespeare wrote *"One touch of nature makes the whole world akin"*. Lord Byron was moved to write *"In her starry shade of dim and solitary loveliness I learn the language of another world"*. St Francis of Assisi observed that the land is *"our Sister, Mother Earth, who sustains and governs us"*. Likewise, in 1836 Ralph W Emerson wrote *"Behind nature, throughout nature, Spirit is present".*

In 'No Destination' Satish Kumar described finding *"...a tree that looked like a Buddha...the tree is my church, the tree is my temple, the tree is my poem and my prayer."* Two illustrations here demonstrate his point, showing how trees can resemble dragons, people, animals and so on. In fact, the range and frequency of such perceived forms is limited only by our imagination. Nature is constantly reaching out to us for recognition, enticing us to reach beyond outer appearances to the real essence within.

❖❖❖❖❖❖❖❖❖❖❖❖❖❖❖❖❖❖❖❖❖❖❖❖❖❖

"When the tree were enchanted there was hope for the trees."

From an old Welsh triad

❖❖❖❖❖❖❖❖❖❖❖❖❖❖❖❖❖❖❖❖❖❖❖❖❖❖

The same can be said for perceiving breast-shaped hills (such as in Pilgrimages 3 and 6) and seeing faces staring at you from megaliths (as on Pilgrimages 3 and 10). Ancient stones with votive holes, symbolic of the vulva of the Earth Goddess, can be seen on Pilgrimages 4 and 10. On the north face of the Agglestone, the sacred destination of Pilgrimage 10, can be seen a huge face overlooking the heath. The locality has Druidic folklore, which is hardly surprising when one

On a tree this fungi takes on the form of a wise sage, with garb and head-dress. Below a finger points the way.

sees the huge facial features timelessly surveying the land.

To begin to perceive such forms in hills, stones and trees is to cross a threshold to lands anew, both physically and psychologically.

Many races and mystics throughout the ages have regarded the land as a mirror of the Divine. The Australian Aborigines see themselves and their forebears as living participants of the myths of their landscape. They see images of their gods, ancestors and the Earth Spirit all around them. Aboriginal poet Kevin Gilbert states *"...I AM Ayre's Rock ...the very soul sustenance."* An Aborigine elder called Nosepeg once explained to anthropologists that an outcrop of boulders they stood at was more than it seemed: "They are an old man and his wives, huddled

The Dragon Tree, Woodlands, rising from the earth, complete with eyes, mouth, nostrils and tongue. (See SD p230-234)

together for warmth." Every atom of the Aboriginal landscape is the embodiment of some spirit, ancestor or myth. In other words, THE LAND LIVES.

Paul Devereux in 'Re-Visioning the Earth', calls Nature the "Dream Maker" and urges us to *"...animate the landscape around you..."* to literally *"live the Dreamtime".* Amongst other things, pilgrimage is about RECEIVING FROM THE LAND THAT WHICH IT IS COMMUNICATING TO US. The landscape and it's sacred sites are places of inspiration, where the human spirit is temporarily set free. The land is a repository of sacred images which, once perceived, will leap out at you from rock, tree, cloud and hill alike. And walking is the ideal conduit for such an awakening. *"The simplest way to explore Gaia is on foot"* states scientist James Lovelock, *"How else can you easily be part of her ambience."*

Nature is an allegory of spiritual dimensions. Japanese Zen philosopher Daisetz Suzuki puts it thus: *"The earth is Man's very body ...the great educator and great disciplinarian."* This magically perceived landscape can be a crucible for self-change. Ancient

sacred sites are indeed capsules of eternity and centres of reconciliation. If we treat geography as imagination then a whole genesis of wonder unfolds. Yet we can only perceive outside what is within. If we reach out to the Earth Spirit, then the Earth will respond. A deep love and respect for the Earth can but only enhance one's life and can certainly add new dimensions to pilgrimage.

We walk on a skin, not a crust of rock. We walk on the Earth as honoured guests, not gatecrashers. We walk on the Earth as its stewards, not as pillagers. We walk on the Earth as tenants, not as its owners. So take your soul for a journey into the landscape, for we are all, ultimately, part of it. Dorset is infused with ancient wisdom and myth, if we would have eyes to see. So, as you walk across the land using this guide, take heed of the wisdom of the land being revealed to you. Be mindful not to dismiss 'co-incidences' and 'good fortune' and other subtle workings of the Earth Spirit. For the land has been awaiting your return.

An isolated path passing through a Dorset Wood. It epitomises the connection one can achieve with nature.

FIVE

SETTING OUT - FOLLOW THE YELLOW BRICK ROAD

'Flower – like the heels of the wanderer,
His body groweth and is fruitful,
All his sins disappear,
Slain by the toll of his journeying.' From the Indian Vedas

There are few things in life that are free, happily walking is one of them. Not only is it excellent exercise it also refreshes the mind and body. Like other forms of exercise 'feel good' chemicals are released by the brain which lift our spirits and better help us cope with this fast technological world in which we now live. What could be better than walking through a bluebell wood on a warm sunny spring day, the only noise being the rustle of leaves, the buzz of bees and the chatter of birds above.

Our walks are not circular, you will therefore need to be picked up or leave a car at the finish, although it is possible to use public transport in some instances. Another option is to go by bike. Drive to the finish, cycle to the start along the nearest convenient roads, safely secure your bike/s and at the end of the walk return to collect them. For those wishing to split the pilgrimage we have suggested a suitable halfway point in the introduction to each walk.

We cannot really imagine how early pilgrims must have fared, or what shoes they possessed, if any, providing little or no support or protection with conditions underfoot nothing more than wet, rutted stone tracks. How they must have suffered also from the cold and wet.

The modern day pilgrim is much more fortunate, and whilst it is not necessary to purchase special clothing and equipment if you do it will only increase your comfort and enjoyment. The most important area is your footwear. It is essential to wear comfortable, well-treaded boots, shoes or sandals and if wet or muddy they must be waterproof.

When buying, the most expensive is not always the best but it is worth paying the extra cost for Gore-Tex lined boots, which not only keep your feet dry from the outside but wick moisture from the inside out. Care of boots is also very important; those with Gore-Tex linings generally only need washing after use and then treating with ordinary boot polish, whilst most of the others need to be waxed regularly either by a spray or solid wax paying special attention to the seams. If buying for the first time it is advisable, and we are speaking from experience, to buy a half size larger than your normal shoe size, not only to accommodate thicker socks but also to remain comfortable if your feet should become swollen. High tech' boots are now coming onto the market in ever increasing numbers and well worth investigating especially lightweight versions for hard summer surfaces. We are often asked is it better to wear one or two pairs of socks, personally it makes no difference although some people find that wearing two pairs prevents blisters. Our preference is to wear one pair the weight depending upon the weather. We prefer wool and go for socks that are padded against abrasion, have Lycra ankle support to

23

prevent movement and smooth toe seams, they are expensive but they extremely comfortable and made to last.

Layered clothing is best, with a shirt or thermal vest, a fleece top and a waterproof/windproof jacket. Light-weight, quick drying trousers are preferable to shorts and jeans. We also prefer to wear gaiters, not only do they protect your ankles and keep your trousers clean they help prevent water entering the top of your boots.

A small rucksack or shoulder bag is an essential item as you will need to carry sufficient liquid especially on the pilgrimages where there are no pubs or tea-rooms on route. It is also advisable to have with you the relevant Ordnance Survey maps; these are listed at the start of each walk. Other useful items are a penknife, a watch, spare boot laces, a torch, money, a compass, sun cream, a sun hat and sunglasses. A walking stick is more than useful as it can be used to clear brambles and nettles, test the stability of the ground ahead and waved in the air if necessary to deter livestock.

The 'Rights of Way Act', which came into force on August 13th 1990, has much improved the rights of walkers; it was a massive step forward in path protection. The Act requires occupiers who disturb the land to make good the surface within 24 hours of the disturbance or 2 weeks if the disturbance is the first one for a particular crop. Where no width is recorded the minimum for a path must be 1 metre and 2 metres for a bridleway and the exact line of the path must be apparent on the ground. Furthermore the occupier must prevent crops growing on, or encroaching onto the path.

Any person using a public footpath has the right to remove as much of the obstruction as necessary to allow him or her to pass, but not to cause wilful damage to property. If the obstruction cannot be removed the walker is entitled to leave the path and walk round it, causing no more damage than is necessary. If the path has been sown with crops you are entitled to follow the route even if it means treading on the crop. Hopefully you will not experience any problems with the routes in this book but if you do you should report them to the 'Rights of Way' department at County Hall Dorchester. (Telephone: 01305 224463)

Where safe to do so keep to the right-hand side of the road in the absence of pavements. Always remember that wherever you go in the countryside, always follow the code. Do not light fires, fasten all gates, keep dogs under control and always on a lead where livestock are present. Take your litter home, do not pick wild flowers or dig up plants.

Leave nothing but footprints take nothing but memories

The stile, over ancient stone wall leading into woods, captures the spirit of pilgrimage – stepping into the unknown.

Six

RETURNING - SHOW ME THE WAY TO GO HOME

"This is my play's last scene,
Here heavens appoint
My pilgrimages last mile."

From 'Holy Sonnet No. 1', John Donne (1572 – 1631).

Returning home from a pilgrimage can be a strange time. Having isolated ourselves on our quest, and perhaps having experienced wonderful things, the mundane world can often seem dull and meaningless. For some a culture shock may occur, even after just a day away from city and town. One cannot relate to shopping at the supermarket, for one is still 'out there' or 'off somewhere'.

Yet it is pointless to bemoan that your beautiful pilgrimage has ended, or that you hate being back, and cannot wait until the next one, etc. As well as being self-destructive, you are in fact tarnishing and degrading the very pilgrimage journey itself. Why go on a journey at all if you feel worse than before you left?

However, the very ideal of pilgrimage (apart from the obvious by-product of healthy exercise) is to gain insights to enhance our everyday lives and give us understandings of some of life's personal issues. The act of pilgrimage exposes us to the process of revelation, which can enthuse our normal lives with wisdom and hope.

It is important that the post-pilgrimage period does not turn into some sort of aftermath, with that 'Boxing-day feeling', a let down, an anticlimax no less. For there is much to be gained if a time of reflection, an inner pilgrimage, follows the outer one. What were your profound experiences en route and at the sacred sites you visited? What moved you, and why? What disappointments did you experience, and why? Did your expectations in fact set you up for those disappointments? (Perhaps it is best to approach pilgrimage with as few preconceptions as possible). Were you disillusioned whilst on your journey, or since your return, and again try to ask yourself why? What inner feelings were brought out of the cupboard with your boots?

On pilgrimage we get clues to what lies in people's hearts, both our own and of those we encounter. We can also treat chance meetings on our journey as meaningful and, likewise, can employ a similar process with those mysterious 'co-incidences' that crop up in our daily lives. 'Chance' meetings and those 'pieces of luck' (both 'good' and 'bad') all help weave our lives into an intricate web, a web that links everything and everyone on this planet. We create memories every moment of our lives and these can later be employed, with hindsight, to enrich our hearts and minds. Sometimes a so-called 'co-incidence' can later be seen to have changed the direction of one's entire life.

Whether you can approach this guide as a tool for pleasant days out in the countryside or an aid to something deeper is really up to you. We do not really mind which one

Wooden statue of the pilgrim St. James, late 15th century, in the timber roof at Bere Regis church.

quest then we are searching for a Holy Grail hidden within ourselves. We may get fleeting glimpses of the Chalice on pilgrimages, at a sacred site, on lonely hilltops and other places of spiritual power. Yet it is back at home that the effects of any cathartic experiences will manifest themselves. Your immersion into daily life is the true test of how a pilgrimage may have changed you.

So, as you unpack your rucksack, will you be discarding unwanted mental and emotional baggage too? Perhaps your first pilgrimage or two may not contain any thunderous revelations or earth-shattering shifts of the mind. Yet perhaps, just perhaps, a spark may have been ignited. You may feel an inner thirst that is not easily quenched. You may get the urge to explore that which normally lies hidden within, previously unchallenged, safely tucked away. This something, this Holy Grail, is different for each person on the earth. We hope this guide helps lead you to yours.

you adopt. But to some this book will be seen not only as a walking guide, but as a catalyst, hopefully, to reach greater horizons and explore new *inner* landscapes. We hope the reader not only encounters the stillness of the land and its sacred sites, but also that still place that resides within all of us. This inner peace and calm, especially if reached in a traffic jam or midst the supermarket scrum, can turn our everyday live into pilgrimage. Life is about perceptions and we create our personal film every second. We direct it, star in it and write the script. It is entirely up to each one of us to create either a Shakespearean tragedy or an action adventure.

Pilgrimage can be a key to unlock the doors of our perceptions and awareness. The toughest part of a pilgrimage may to many commence when we take our boots off. All that preceded that moment may have in fact been just the beginning, a prelude to our return. If life is indeed a pilgrimage, then to where are we heading and from whence have we come? What is our destination in life and how shall we travel there? If life be a

❖❖❖❖❖❖❖❖❖❖❖❖❖❖❖❖❖❖❖❖❖❖❖❖❖

"Dear has been the pilgrimage before going to meet death"
9th C. Irish hermit.

❖❖❖❖❖❖❖❖❖❖❖❖❖❖❖❖❖❖❖❖❖❖❖❖❖

SYMBOLS USED IN THE PILGRIMS MAP

pilgrimage route, and direction of walk

intersection of other paths and roads

woods on or close to route

round barrows (tumuli)

long barrows

stone circles

earthworks, fortifications, henges, etc

ancient stones (standing & fallen)

ancient crosses (stone)

churches and chapels

other places of interest: obelisks, wells, trees, etc

O.S. trig. point

ponds and lakes

camp sites (those on route only)

pubs and inns

steep road gradients

post office/village stores

route goes under/over railway line

view points (selected)

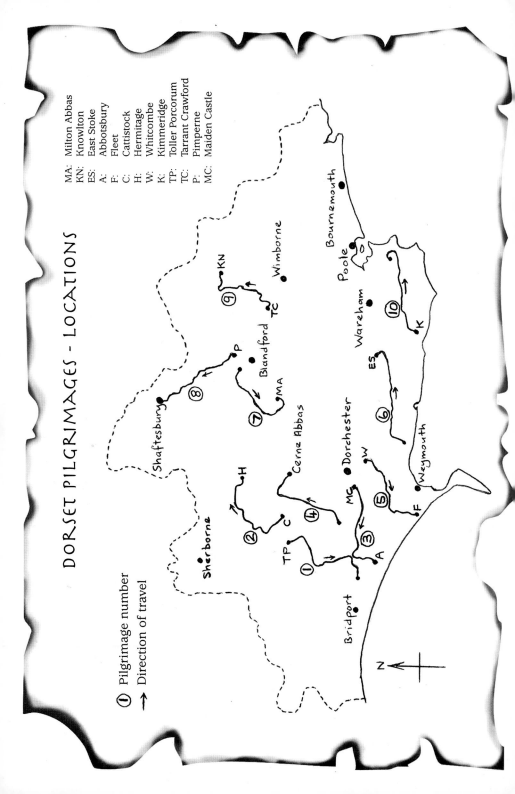

DORSET PILGRIMAGES - LOCATIONS

Ⓘ Pilgrimage number
→ Direction of travel

MA: Milton Abbas
KN: Knowlton
ES: East Stoke
A: Abbotsbury
F: Fleet
C: Cattistock
H: Hermitage
W: Whitcombe
K: Kimmeridge
TP: Toller Porcorum
TC: Tarrant Crawford
P: Pimperne
MC: Maiden Castle

TO THE HOLY CHAPEL IN THE WOODS

Toller Porcorum is signposted from the A356 Maiden Newton to Crewkerne road about a mile west of Maiden Newton.

OS Maps: Landranger 194, Explorer 117 and Outdoor Leisure 15. Reference: 564/979.

Approximate distance:13 miles (optional 14 miles). The Helstone is ideal for a split walk.

A little demanding at times this very hilly walk starts from Toller Porcorum, Toller meaning a brook in a steep valley Porcorum (of the Pigs). It appears in the Doomsday Book of 1086 as Tolre and was known as Swynestolre or Hogstolre. From here we head south to Toller Fratrum (of the Brothers). Our pilgrimage continues through the hamlets of Wynford Eagle and West Compton before descending Whatcombe Down to reach Littlebredy and the Kingston Russell Stone Circle finally ending our pilgrimage at the remains of St Luke's Chapel. As there are no refreshment stops on route make sure you carry ample supplies with you, especially water.

The church of St Andrew and St Peter in fact stands on an ancient sacred site. Note, for instance, the circular churchyard wall, indicating a round mound of Pre-Christian date. The churches at Church Knowle (Pilgrimage 10) and Knowlton (Pilgrimage 9) stand on similar prehistoric places. On the north side, sections of the wall fell into School Lane some years ago, exposing a still older wall and two upright standing stones. The site may have originally been a stone circle. The two megaliths have been remounted at the east gate and aptly named Peter and Andrew. A ley alignment runs up from Powerstock, through Toller Porcorum church then north-east via other sites to Old Sarum, at Salisbury. Toller Porcorum is a wonderful example of the Christianisation of an ancient sacred site (see AS fig 12 for

Toller Porcorum church, built on a prehistoric megalithic site.

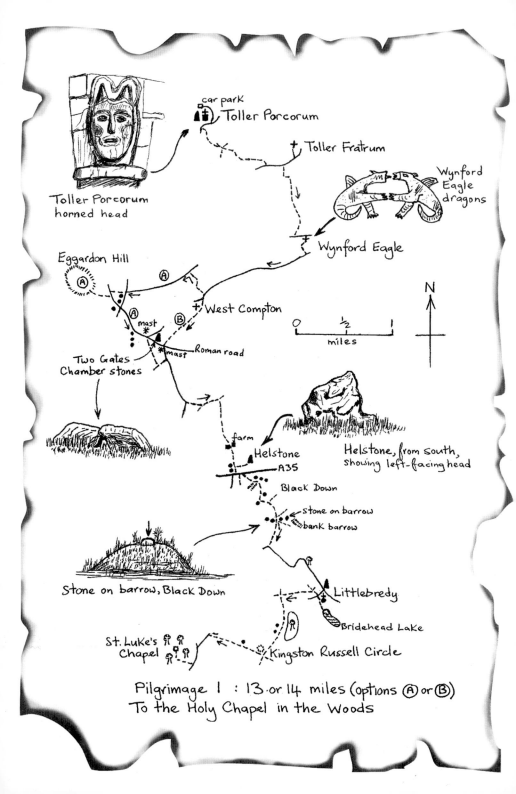

car park

Toller Porcorum

Toller Fratrum

Wynford Eagle dragons

Toller Porcorum horned head

Wynford Eagle

Eggardon Hill

Ⓐ

Ⓐ

Ⓐ

mast

Ⓑ

West Compton

N

0   ½   1
miles

Two Gates Chamber stones

mast

Roman road

farm

Helstone

Helstone, from south, showing left-facing head

A35

Black Down

stone on barrow

bank barrow

Stone on barrow, Black Down

Littlebredy

Bridehead Lake

St. Luke's Chapel

Kingston Russell Circle

Pilgrimage 1 : 13 or 14 miles (options Ⓐ or Ⓑ)
To the Holy Chapel in the Woods

ley map). Note the winged gargoyles up the 13-14th century tower and some other carved heads on the exterior stonework.

Inside, note the spirals and ram's head with horns on the Norman font. Ancient symbolism is present here. Spirals have been found on Mesolithic cave paintings and in Neolithic tombs, whilst horned creatures such as rams and bulls gave rise to many ancient fertility cults (see SD fig.18 for drawings of this interesting font). Note also the small horned head carved at the base of the arch near the altar. We will encounter many such heads in Christian architecture on the 10 pilgrimages, testament to one of the most enduring images of Celtic and earlier times –

One of the two megaliths at Toller Porcorum.

Under the aqueduct near Toller Fratrum.

the horned god. He was of course transformed into the devil for political purposes as the Church denounced all gods and goddesses of cultures it sought to convert. Some researchers have suggested Toller Porcorum was home to the Knights Templars.

After visiting the church turn right up through the village, over the dis-used railway line and take the next left into Frogmore Lane. Walk up, round and just before the entrance to the farm keep straight ahead onto the bridleway signposted, Toller Fratrum 1. Go down to the gate at the bottom of this attractive but often muddy track then bear right to the little bridge, cross the stream and stile into the field opposite and head up to the stile in the top corner. Bearing slightly right make your way down to the gate then up and over the field to the gate on the far side and across to the stile turning left onto the track. Continue walking, up past the dwelling, under the aqueduct and down towards Toller Fratrum. To visit the church take the first turning on the left.

Toller Fratum is a place that time seems to have forgotten, a tiny cluster of 16-17th century thatched cottages, a farm and tiny chapel. These buildings and the ancient stone walls hereabouts owe their foundation to the Knights Hospitallers, or The Knights of St John

The church of St. Basil, Toller Fratrum.

The saxon font at Toller Fratrum, with unusual carvings.

of Jerusalem. They are the 'Fratres' or brothers of the place name. They were an esoteric order, similar to the Templars, who provided healing and aid to Holy Land pilgrims. They used unorthodox healing techniques from the East, and were regarded with suspicion by the church. They were established in this isolated spot from perhaps as early as 12th C to the Dissolution of 1539. The former Manor house may have been rebuilt in Tudor times when the Knights were driven from Rhodes by the Turks. Note the esoteric stonework, such as the twisted chimneys and the monkey and dragon.

The nearby church of St Basil owes its unusual dedication to St Basil the Great (c. 325-379) of Constantinople and Athens. He built hospitals, almshouses and set up soup kitchens for the poor. It is said that at his funeral 'Catholics, pagans and strangers alike' paid homage to him, such was his reputation for kindness and helping the sick and destitute. The dedication at this church is only too appropriate at a Knights Hospitallers locality.

The church was rebuilt in the 19th century but note the two medieval heads either side of the door. Inside there are two unique relics. The font is 11-12th century and has scenes of severed heads, women, children and a monster with two bodies and only one head. Ancient esoteric symbolism is obvious here. Behind the altar, set onto the wall, is a unique stone carving, dated 11th century, displaying what is generally regarded as Mary Magdalene washing Christ's feet. She is very forlorn and small, out of scale with Christ's figure. Some writers have interpreted the scene as representing the replacement of older pagan ways (as Mary Magdalene is equated with the Earth Goddess Kali) by Christianity. It marks the passing of the Aries age of the Goddess into the Piscean age of Christianity.

Retrace your steps a few paces up hill and join the bridleway on the left signposted to Wynford Eagle. The track rises fairly steeply above the village and into a field at the top. Bearing right walk up and over the rise making for the little gate in the boundary. Keep straight ahead in the direction of the fingerpost following the track all the way down to the village and turn left walking as far as the church.

The 11th century carving at Toller Fratrum

Wynford Eagle church was built in 1840 to replace an older one. A clue to the site being ancient is a ley line discovered recently by Andrew Lane, who plots an alignment running from the cross at Maiden Newton to Beacon Knap, via Wynford Eagle church and other sites. As with many other ley churches we find dragon symbolism. To the left of the porch a large carved stone depicts two opposing dragons. The stone is thought to be 11th century, probably a tymparnum of a door lintel of the previous church here. The dragons are two wyverns and fighting dragons such as this are mentioned in many Celtic and Nordic myths (see SD Chapter 3). Inside the church is a surviving 15th century chancel arch and a 13th century font (when locked, keys at nearby Wynford House).

From the church cross the stile into the field and keep straight ahead to the stile on the far side turning left in the field, cross the bridge, go up to the lane and turn right. Keep to this peaceful lane for the mile and a half walk to West Compton, forking left at the junction down to the hamlet. Look for the narrow grass path on the right and walk up to the church, sadly now closed and in a state of disrepair.

The Tymparnum at Wynford Eagle from Hutchins, 1774.

The church at West Compton.

The church is on a former Saxon site, although the oldest relic now is probably a memorial stone set into the exterior wall at the east end, dated 1627. It has been shown previously (AS fig. 128) how the church stands on a ley running from Two Gates Stones, encountered shortly, up to Old Sarum, at Salisbury, via Child Okeford, Belchalwell and Okeford Fitzpaine (all in Pilgrimage 7).

Walk round to the far side and pick up the grass path which rises up over the landscaped area to a stile in the left-hand corner after which a small fenced path and stile funnel you into a large field. Keep straight ahead on this gently rising field path leading to a stile beside a gate, and on to another, finally crossing one last field before reaching a little gate allowing access to the lane.

Just before the lane look for the line of three telegraph poles to your right (west). In between the two nearest are two large prone megaliths, easy to see if there are no crops in the field. These are the Two Gates Stones, the remains of a Neolithic chambered tomb, probably over 5000 years old.

Go straight across into the lane opposite walking until you reach the right-hand bend at which point keep straight ahead on the grass covered country road which leads to a gate. Turn left onto the track and follow it all the way down the hillside turning right onto the farm track at the bottom. Keep straight ahead between the farm buildings and up the drive to the road.

Just before the road look for the Helstone in the field to the east, accessible by a track to its south. This is one of Dorset's finest megaliths and well worth the short detour. Over 10 feet of stone rises from the ground, although a pronounced lean to the south reduces the height. Note the ledge at the east end, possibly used in the distant past for seating. At the one end of the ledge is a deep hole, Earth Goddess vulvic symbolism, with a votive-offering ledge (see Nine Stones, Harpstone and Rempstone for similar holes, all in this guide). On the south side of the stone is a huge left-facing head profile, with eye, nose and mouth. Features such as these have been found on many of the megaliths at Avebury by Dr Terence Meaden. Peter Knight has discovered other Dorset examples, such as at The Grey Mare long barrow and the Hellstone (both Pilgrimage 3) and the Nine

The Two Gates Stones, the remains of a Neolithic Tomb.

(below/left) The north side of The Helstone. The arrow marks the vulvar hole and votive ledge.

(below/right) The south face of The Helstone, showing the left-facing head in the morning sun (compare with AS Plate 72: slightly different sun angle.)

Stones (Pilgrimage 4). The face here at the Helstone is only visible in the morning, with the sun's rays shining obliquely from the east to south-east.

Note the two Bronze Age barrows on the right just before the road is reached. Seen from the Helstone they mark out sunsets on the sacred festivals of Imbolc (early February) and Samhain (November 1).

After carefully crossing the busy A35 turn left and join the bridleway signposted through a small gate which rises up a concrete track to a farm gate. Pass through and bear right towards the Long Barrow turning left by the tumuli and go down the field to the gate. Follow the track beyond to the gate then head up the field to the small gate at the top and immediately turn right through the wide gate and go down the sunken track ahead. Take time to enjoy the lovely views whilst descending Whatcombe Down. Bear right through a gate then a second before passing farm buildings on the right (presently to the left around a small enclosed field). Continue down through a couple more gates finally turning left into the lane.

Upon reaching Littlebredy turn right at the shelter (noting the ley stone next to it. See AS plate 5). Walk down towards the church turning right across the grass to the stile. For a short but worthwhile diversion follow the path on the left, past the church of St Michael's and All Angels and go down across the grass to the lake, a lovely peaceful place to rest awhile.

(below) The thatched cottages on the approach to Littlebredy church.

St Michael's church nestles in a valley, overlooking woods, a stone's throw from the beautiful lake and waterfall. The church was largely restored and rebuilt in 1850, but some of the older stonework remains. The tower is 14th century, supporting the 19th century spire. The porch, vestry doorway and piscina are 13-14th century, as too some partly restored windows. Of interest is the wall monument to William Williams, dated 1839, who was the Provincial Grand Mason. The monument has Masonic emblems. Note too the six carved angels near the altar.

(above) Littlebredy church. Like many St. Michael churches, it stands on a ley line.

The lion gargoyle, close to ground level, Littlebredy church.

In the churchyard blocks of stone can be found here and there and may point to a pre-Christian site. Churches dedicated to St Michael (the dragon-slayer) are common on ley lines (the dragon lines of old). Two leys pass through the church and/or the markstone in the village, described previously (see AS figs. 52 and 89).

To the south of the church is Bridehead Lake, the source of the River Bride. Several springs bubble up from beneath the earth under the waters and the site would have been highly venerated in prehistoric to Romano-British times. A glance at the OS map shows an encirclement of ancient sites on the surrounding hills, such as settlements, enclosures,

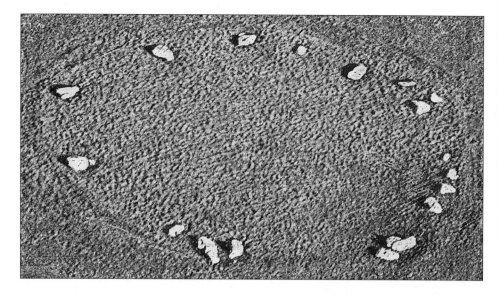

Kingston Russell Stone Circle.

tumuli and megalithic sites. The name Bride comes from St Bride, the saint who succeeded the ancient goddess Brighid or Brigit.

Having returned to the road and crossed to the stile bear right over the field to the stile in the hedge opposite after which veer left down the hillside making for the gap in the hedge. Bear right for a short distance (can be wet) crossing both stiles and small brook to reach the field on the left. Bearing slightly right walk up and over the field making for the pair of stiles in the far hedge. Turn left into the field walking all the way round the boundary until you reach the point where a well-trodden path drops down to a small metal gate on the right.

Bear left up this rather uneven and often wet field making for the gate in the top hedge, pass through and bear left up and over the rise to another gate. Keep close to the edge of the wood for a while and then climb the hill making for the left-hand side of the earth works (Hut Circle) and go across to the gate and into the field bearing left to reach Kingston Russell Circle.

The Kingston Russell Stone Circle is Dorset's largest Bronze Age circle, 18 stones enclosing an area 90 x 80 feet. Most are of the hard conglomerate sarsen type, full of intensely hard pebbles and angular flints. All the stones are prone and may have always been. Many other stone circles around Britain were laid out with stones lying on the ground. The circle's location was chosen with great care, enabling distant views of hills and skylines. From the circle the winter solstice sun rises over the Grey Mare and Her Colts long barrow, seen to the SE through the gaps in the hedgerow. To the east the equinox sun rises over the hill capped by the Hardy Monument, a hill festooned with

tumuli. Other astronomical sight lines occur as well as a lunar event (see AS pages 126-8 for further details).

Beautiful grounds and waterfall south of Littlebredy church.

Not suprisingly, some ley lines pass through or close to the circle (see AS figs. 77 and 88) and Peter Knight has previously suggested a processional way passing by the circle linking it to several sites between here and the Hellstone to the east. It is Dorset's most isolated stone circle, a place to reflect and to personally experience sunrises and sunsets at a sacred site.

❖❖❖❖❖❖❖❖❖❖❖❖❖❖❖❖❖❖❖❖❖❖❖❖❖

My feet are heavy, the journey has been long,
Up hill and along ridge I have trudged,
Past ancestral mounds, silent and dark.
The way ahead is fading into oblivion,
As darkness creeps over the land like
An insatiable twilight dragon,
Who eats the land, yet births the stars.
I am summoned by the Men of Stone.

There you are, old friends of mine,
Cold to the touch, yet with spirits of fire.
The pilgrimage is achieved, my quest it be done,
We are as one at the setting of the sun,
Immersed in this perfect moment in time.
Yet it is a moment beyond time.....
Tell me, stones, how can my mind grasp eternity?
("Kingston Russell Sunset", Peter Knight, 1999).

❖❖❖❖❖❖❖❖❖❖❖❖❖❖❖❖❖❖❖❖❖❖❖❖

Bridehead Lake, near Littlebredy church.

From here we turn right beside the hedge line to the gate on the far side maintaining direction along the track and through another gate. (Lovely distant views of Golden Cap). Walk until you reach the gate on the left, enter the field and bear right down to the gate, out onto the tarred drive and turn left. After dropping down past Ashley Dairy walk up the lane ahead turning right immediately after the thatched cottage, past the farm buildings and into the field.

Keeping close to the right-hand hedge walk until you reach the gate, pass through and turn right going round beside the hedge until you come to the stile then follow the twisting path down through the bluebell wood to reach the chapel. The path behind the arch will bring you back to the road.

The atmospheric remains of St Luke's chapel are surrounded by woodland and overlook a small ravine through which a stream meanders, 50 feet below. The wall and tall arch are all that survive of a 13-14th century Cistercian cell, whose monks chose an ideal setting for isolated contemplation. Some researchers have suggested that the chapel was used by the Knight's Templars, the esoteric order who are known to have been in Dorset. The Templars are associated with chapels built on places of powerful earth energies and Peter Knight has dowsed strong energies flowing through the arch to the altar and cross. Of a more recent date the tombs of Olga and David Milne-Watson can be seen. They built Ashley Chase House, to the south-east of here. The altar was also erected by them from the original chapel stones. Note also the stone heads on the arch walls.

At the chapel and its tranquil woods we can perhaps reflect on the day's pilgrimage and know that around 700 years ago, if not earlier, our ancestors were likewise journeying here, following their own faith and connecting with the Divine aspects of nature.

Sacred, sacrosanct, sanctuary
In the ruins of what was sacred space that we need back,
But now the breeze stirs, and when we slow our steps,
Where stone breathes we can receive its whispered gift again
(Extract from "The Sacred Way", by Jay Ramsey).

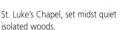
St. Luke's Chapel, set midst quiet isolated woods.

Pilgrimage 2: 14 miles
Nine Churches to the Holy Well

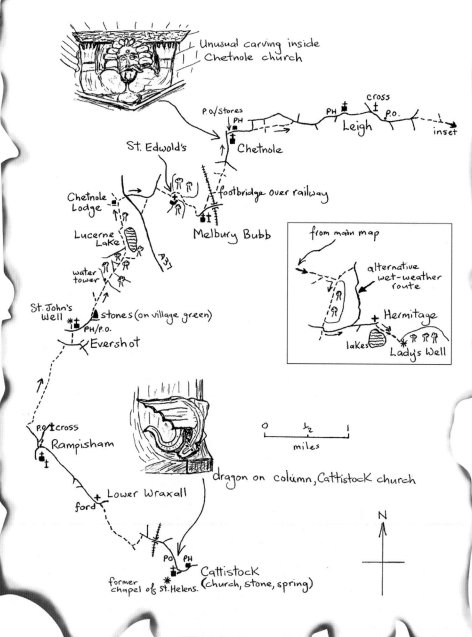

Unusual carving inside Chetnole church

P.O./stores

PH

Chetnole

Leigh

cross

P.O.

inset

St. Edwold's

footbridge over railway

Chetnole Lodge

Lucerne Lake

Melbury Bubb

A37

water tower

St. John's Well

stones (on village green)

PH/P.O.

Evershot

from main map

alternative wet-weather route

Hermitage

lakes

Lady's Well

P.O./cross

Rampisham

0   ½   1
miles

dragon on column, Cattistock church

Lower Wraxall

ford

Po   PH

Cattistock (church, stone, spring)

former chapel of St. Helens.

N

PILGRIMAGE TWO

ᴎιɴε Cʜᴜʀᴄʜεꜱ Tᴏ Tʜε Hᴏʟᴜ ᴡεʟʟ

A fairly long but very enjoyable hike on a mix of peaceful country lanes, field paths and bridleways. The walk takes you to the peaceful village of Evershot, referred to as Evershead by Thomas Hardy in his novel TESS OF THE D'URBERVILLES. The bridleway near the end of the walk which leads to Hermitage can be extremely muddy in all but the summer months. The Acorn Inn at Evershot is the first refreshment stop and towards the end of the walk there are pubs at Chetnole and Leigh.

Start from Cattistock parking anywhere in the village.

OS Maps: Landranger 194 and Explorer 117.
Reference: 592/997.

Approximate distance:
14 miles. Evershot is probably the best place for a split walk.

Earthworks on Castle Hill and traces of a hamlet, older than the English throne, show that Cattistock has long been inhabited. Athelstan, first King of All England, gave the land to the monks in return for prayers. However, a relic of more ancient times still exists in the village today. At the Fox and Hounds pub, note the large stone at the corner, partially entombed by the building. It is believed that the stone is an original ley marker, as it has been demonstrated previously (AS Figs. 12 & 36) how Cattistock lies on not one, but two ley lines, one of which goes all the way to Old Sarum near Salisbury.

left: The spring in the churchyard at Cattistock.

right: One of the unusual carvings on the west side of Cattistock church

Walk now to the nearby church of St Peter and St Paul. As you enter the churchyard bear left and follow the path as it descends sharply.

On the left will be found a shrine where a spring issues from the earth. Although the structure is modern the spring is ancient and may have been the original spiritual focus of the area. Springs and wells were seen by ancient peoples as places where the elixir of life flowed from the body of the Earth Mother. St Helen is one of several female saints that took over from healing spring/well goddesses. A chapel dedicated to her formerly stood just ½ mile SSW of here (grid ref. 589/993), indicating a holy spring locality. The church had a major rebuild in 1857, although some of the earliest 15th century fabric can still be found in some of the windows, the walls of the chancels and some carvings and statues. Before entering the church descend the steps on the right to find some statues of a knight and St. Peter. Above the wooden door nearby, note the Green Man, low down for close inspection of this ancient image. As you go in, note the small sleeping dragons in front of you at the base of the columns. A huge painting of St George slaying the dragon rises above the font. The pulpit has a dragon and a winged bull, more vestiges of pre-Christian symbolism. Above the display of the church's history can be found a carving, in wood, of the Green Man, another ancient pagan fertility symbol, seen elsewhere at Evershot, Mappowder and Christchurch Priory (see SD for photos of relics inside the church). Cattistock is a classic example of a synthesis of the Christianisation of a sacred place, an assemblage of pagan-carvings, and a ley line site.

The church at Lower Wraxall.

Leave the churchyard by the north gate, walk up through the village, over the railway line turning left when you reach Wraxall Lane. Follow this un-made by-way up to the junction then turn right walking until you reach the ford at Lower Wraxall. The name derives from 'Wraxhall' meaning 'buzzard corner'. Turn left up the hill to the little church of St Mary.

Inside the peaceful church can be found a Norman font and an altered Norman arch at the doorway.

Further on fork right following the lane ahead into Rampisham. Turn left at the junction and walk to the church of St Michael and All Angels.

As with many other churches dedicated to the dragon-slaying saint, the site lies on a ley alignment, crossing the land from Hackthorne Hill to Minterne Parva (see AS fig. 121). The oldest part is the 14/15th century tower. Note the groteques and dragons up the tower, a common feature on ley-line churches. In the churchyard stands an early 16th century cross with an altar tomb incorporated into its base. The cross was once richly decorated with religious scenes, some of which are still faintly visible (see AS Plate 116).

Back at the junction go down the grass track, over the bridge and into the road opposite the post office turning right. Past Broomfield Farm one soon encounters the remains of an ancient cross.

Daffodils around the Medieval stone cross at Rampisham.

St John's Well, Evershot.

One of the Green Man carvings at Evershot church, with foliage coming out of nostrils.

It is thought to be 15th century and has a 4-foot high tapering shaft. On the west is a carving, now much denuded, thought to have been St. Michael standing on a dragon (see AS page 173). To reach Evershot, the village referred to as Evershard by Thomas Hardy in 'Tess of the d'Urbervilles', pilgrims would have followed the lane passing the cross (about 1½ miles), however there is an alternative route which follows a series of field paths.

Return to the village, turn right, walk as the far as the dwellings and just beyond Glebe Farm cottage turn right up the drive to the stile. Cross into the field keeping straight ahead to the bridge and along the path into the trees. Further on fork right up to the stile and climb the field keeping fairly close to the hedge on the right. Pass through the wide farm gate and bear left in the direction of the waymark making for the small gate on the left-hand side of the small wood opposite. Keep straight ahead across the field, to the gate then up to the stile in the corner. Bearing slightly right make for the gap in the far hedge and almost immediately join the short footpath on the right leading to a gate. Walk up the field to the gate on the right in the far top corner. The track leads to a field. Climb the crossing point in the top left-hand corner and stay on the grass strip leading to the lane. Turn right walking until you reach the signposted footpath on the left turning right upon reaching the village. Turn left into Back Lane to visit St John's Well. It is situated in the dip of the lane, on the right-hand side, enclosed by wooden fencing.

This sacred site is overgrown somewhat in summer but possesses a flight of rough stone steps to enable access to the trickling clear water. The spring is in fact one of the sources of the Frome, Dorset's longest river, and from this humble beginning the waters descend and grow into the wide river at Wareham.

Return along the lane to St Osmund's church.

The chief interest here is the collection of fine carvings on the exterior. An angel and gargoyles grace the upper stonework, whilst three carvings of the Green Man decorate the window surrounds. This ancient woodland spirit is commonly found on church architecture and is thought to have been an attempt by the Church to give God's blessing on the crops and fields, using a symbol the peasantry would recognise. Inside the font is 13th century, and look for the 12th century stone figure holding the key of knowledge.

Walk down through the village to the Acorn Hotel, a very good midway stop and, once refreshed, continue down through the village towards the green.

Here one can see a stone seat, nestling under one of the finest holm oaks in England. Ancient folklore speaks of 'three dumb maidens

The stones at Evershot, guarding one of England's finest holm oaks.

St Edwold's, one of England's smallest churches.

dancing on the village green' hereabouts. Are these the 'maidens' in question, in reality three megaliths, now incorporated into the seat? Countless legends across Britain refer to dancing and moving stones. The link to prehistory is confirmed by two leys which intersect at Evershot (see AS figs. 118 and 119). The village held some of the last surviving mumming plays, which featured George and the Dragon, a memory of the 'dragon lines' of old.

Turn left at the stone seat and take the drive ahead into Melbury Park. Further ahead fork right through the deer gate exiting near the house then turn left towards Melbury Osmond, turning right when you reach the second drive on the right which dips between an avenue of trees. After passing Chetnole Lodge carefully cross the busy road turning right then next left for Leigh. Beyond the bend take the turning on the right to Church Farm but before reaching the bottom go through the wide metal gate on the left and bear right across the field towards the tiny church of St Edwold's, reached across the small stone bridge.

Dedicated to Edwold, the younger brother of St Edmund, the Anglican king murdered by the Danes in 870, it measures just 30 feet by 12 feet and is one of the smallest in England. The building dates from the 15th and 17th centuries. Note the gargoyle 'frightener' below the bell turret. (If locked, keys obtainable at farmhouse).

Return to the path and continue into the field behind the church turning left across to the stile. Follow the track up through the woods to the gate climbing the very steep hillside beyond to reach the bridleway at the top. Turn left along the hedge line to the gate in the bottom corner, pass into the field then bear left heading for the gates to the left of the farm buildings afterwards turning right towards the Church of St. Mary at Melbury Bubb.

The name is derived from Bubba, a Saxon resident. The lovely font inside the church is proof enough that a church must have existed here from very early days. It is thought to be 11th century Anglo-Saxon and displays a selection of animals associated with myths of the Celts and Saxons, such as a stag, dolphin, lion, horse and dragon. It is believed that the Normans hollowed out the font, turning all the animals up-side-down. Also of note are the late-11th century windows, in remarkably fine condition.

The font at Melbury Bubb, with inverted animal carvings of Saxon age.

Melbury Bubb church. The tower is 15th century.

Continue through the village and turn left, past a couple of dwellings and almost immediately take the short track leading to a gate and field on the left. Bearing half left cross the field to the gate, go over the bridge and make for the gate on the left then bear left to the stile. Keeping to the right-hand boundary walk all the way round the field, through two gates before reaching the road at Chetnole. Continue ahead towards the village to the church of St Peter.

This pleasant church has remains of 13th-17th century stonework, the tower being 15th century. Note the fine winged dragons up the tower and the two figures opening a demon's mouth. As one enters the church on the left will be seen a carving of a man, apparently holding the roof up. His features are of the Classical-Celtic style and, interestingly, an orb occupies his 'third eye' position on his brow, an overtly Indian symbol. Other carvings displaying this orb can be found at Loders and Witchampton (Pilgrimage 9), both of medieval age, suggesting an intriguing eastern connection. The church also stands on a ley alignment going south to Maiden Castle (see AS fig. 122).

Turn right on the road to Leigh, signposted 1½. Go past the Chetnole Inn, over the narrow bridge and take the next turning right. Almost immediately pass through the gate into the field on the left and continue ahead through the small copse maintaining direction across more stiles before bearing left after the farm buildings to reach the stile and road. Turn right through the village of Leigh.

Stain glass window at Leigh.

At the church of St Andrew are some features of interest. Tall old yews stand in the churchyard, overlooked by winged dragon-like carvings on the 15th century tower. One carving is a Sheela-na-gig, one of only a handful known in Dorset. The female exhibitionist features are an old image symbolic of the fruitfulness of the Earth Mother. Hundreds of Irish churches and castles have such carvings, but they are rarer in England. Others can be found at Studland (Pilgrimage 10) and Sopley, north of Christchurch. Inside the church look for an exquisite image of the sun, surrounded by blue and red, in a stained glass window.

The unusual carving in Chetnole church.

✧✧✧✧✧✧✧✧✧✧✧✧✧✧✧✧✧✧✧✧✧✧✧✧✧✧✧

Sheela-na-gig, high on tower
Displaying life's entrance, hour by hour,
Few gaze up and recognise,
Yet you see it all, through timeless eyes.
Some be offended, some by shocked,
Though you do not intend to mock,
You merely remind us of old earth ways,
Hag wisdom, fertility of land, mystic days.
Teasing unashamed, say, what's that you call?
"At last I be noticed
If tha' don't beat all!"
'Sheela of Leigh' by Peter Knight

✧✧✧✧✧✧✧✧✧✧✧✧✧✧✧✧✧✧✧✧✧✧✧✧✧✧✧.

Continue through the village to the old stone cross.

This fine example of 13th - 15th century work was put together at separate times, and the top cross is 19th century. This wayside cross, passed no doubt by pilgrims in the past, once had carvings of St Christopher and St Michael slaying the poor dragon again, but these are now too eroded to define (for further details see AS page 191).

After passing the cross, go over the bridge and all the way up to the corner and the turning for Hermitage. The Pilgrim's route would have been straight ahead on the bridleway, which can be very muddy and challenging even in early summer. Fortunately present day pilgrims have a second option and can keep on the road to Hermitage albeit a very boring option.

The Sheela-na-gig at Leigh.

51

The track ahead leads to a pair of gates, take the one on the right and follow the fenced path beyond into the copse. Bear left tracking your way along the path, up into the field then bear half-right up and over the rise making for the small metal gate in the far right-hand corner. Maintain your direction to the gate at the bottom of the field then head up to the gate in the hedge at the top and make for the trees where there is a small gate and bridleway beyond. Generally good at the beginning it can become very muddy later making the going hard. There are many wild flowers in the area including primroses and orchids. When you eventually reach the road turn left through Hermitage, forking right at the junction then join the path opposite the church. After skirting the fishing lakes, the path emerges into open fields. Follow the hedge on the right up the hill to where it meets the woods.

The medieval cross at Leigh.

Lady's Well, Hermitage.

Lady's Well lies at the edge of the wood, low stones forming a cover for the rising waters, with a basin nearby. The water would certainly have been drunk by the local pious men who gave Hermitage its name, perhaps even St Edwold himself, who had a cell at Cerne Abbas. It has probably been in use since at least medieval times as a holy place. The well lies directly on a ley running from Clarkham Cross to Bulbarrow via Rawlsbury Camp (see AS fig. 127). A link has already been demonstrated between some sacred wells and leys (see SD pages 104 – 114). Many researchers regard Lady's Wells around the country as Christianisations of former dedications to female pagan goddesses. There is a tradition that High Stoy, ¾ mile to the south, was a place of pilgrimage. There is a path connecting it to Lady's Well, strengthening the argument for the well itself being an ancient pilgrimage destination. The locality is easily the most isolated and modest of the pilgrimage destinations in this guide, a place of quiet contemplation, with just the trees and the trickling water for company.

Dig under:
Where the well is depth, is other,
Is the underworld, the other world, the Earth and Hers
What do you want? What have you brought here?
From 'Sacred Way' by Jay Ramsey.

53

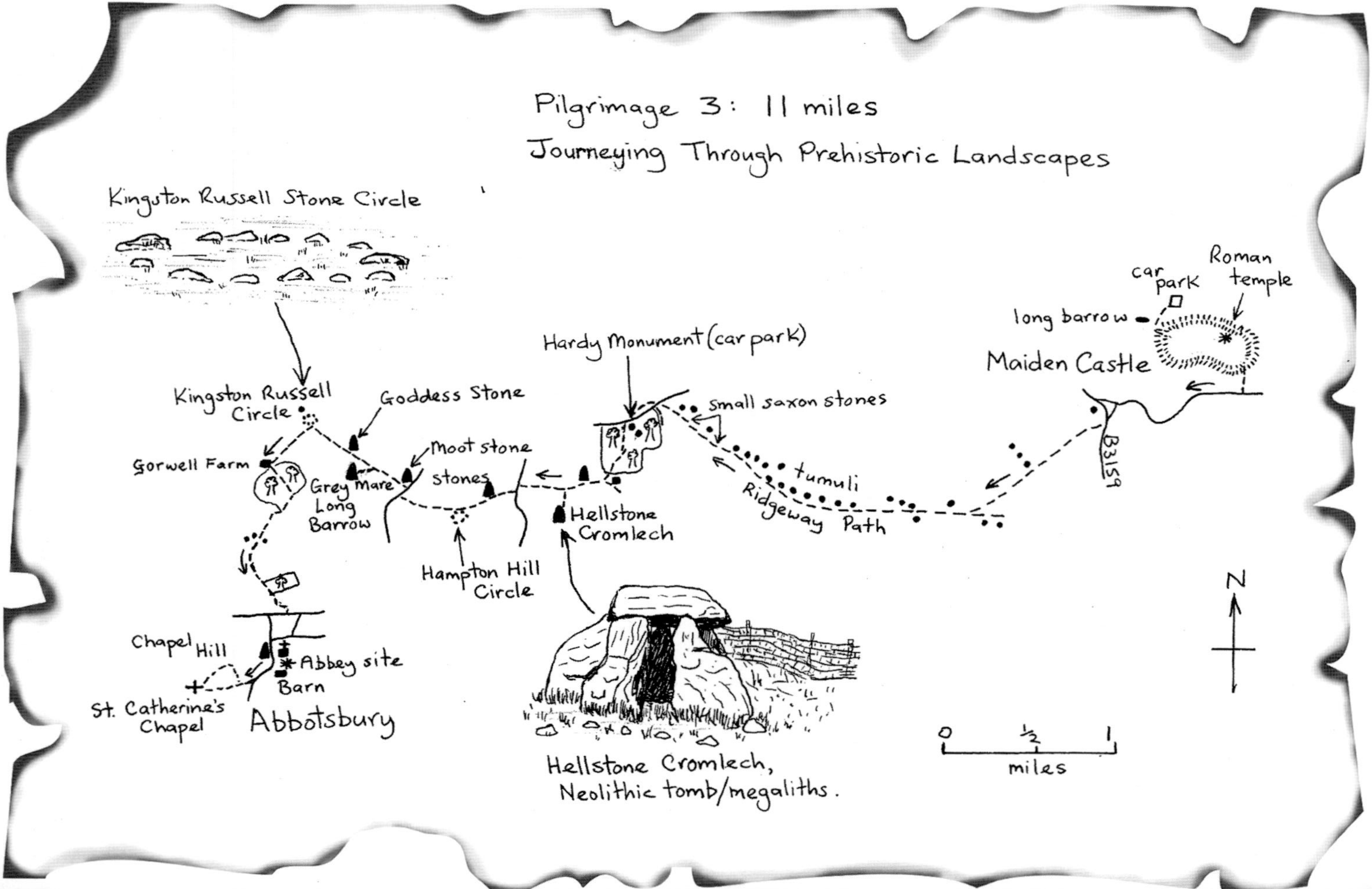

Pilgrimage 3: 11 miles
Journeying Through Prehistoric Landscapes

Kingston Russell Stone Circle

Kingston Russell Stone Circle

Goddess Stone

Moot stone

stones

Hampton Hill Circle

Grey Mare Long Barrow

Kingston Russell Circle

Gorwell Farm

Chapel Hill

St. Catherine's Chapel

Abbey site

Barn

Abbotsbury

Hardy Monument (car park)

Hellstone Cromlech

Hellstone Cromlech, Neolithic tomb/megaliths.

Small saxon stones

tumuli

Ridgeway Path

Maiden Castle

long barrow

car park

Roman temple

B3159

N

0   ½   1
miles

A JOURNEY THROUGH PREHISTORIC LANDSCAPES

Start from the car park at
Maiden Castle.

OS Maps: Landranger 194 and
Outdoor Leisure 15.
Reference: 665/887.

*After leaving Maiden Castle this very enjoyable scenic walk follows the
inland route of the Dorset Coastal Path on Bronkham Hill to reach
Hardy's Monument after which a series of field paths and bridleways guide
you to the Hellstone, the Grey Mare and Her Colts long barrow and
Kingston Russell Stone Circle before descending Tennants Hill and
joining the bridleway down into Abbotsbury. The walk is generally good
underfoot and although hilly in places is not over demanding. As
refreshments on the way are non-existent take your own. There are two
pubs and tea-rooms in Abbotsbury.*

Approximate distance:
11 miles. Hardy's Monument is
ideal for a split walk.

**From the car park head up the main track through the gate
bearing left through the fort to the small gate at the top.**

You ascend through the labyrinthine embankments, originally constructed by the ancient Britons as a ritual processional route and
later modified into defensive structures to protect the hill from the
invading Romans. One's view is restricted through the banks until
suddenly one is at the top, where the vastness of Maiden Castle
becomes apparent. With a length of 3000 feet and covering 120
acres, it is estimated that over 4000 people lived here prior to the

The embankments of Maiden
Castle.

Roman occupation, when the fort fell with a bloody siege. The sheer
magnitude of the hill so affected Thomas Hardy to write:

*"The profile of the whole stupendous ruin, as seen
from a distance a mile eastwards, is clearly cut as that of a
marble inlay. It may be likened to an enormous
many-limbed organism, lying lifeless".*

In 1926 H J Massingham wrote in 'Downland Man', "Maiden
Castle has a solitude that frightened one a little because it is so vast
and calm". The hill is a very ancient sacred place. A Neolithic mound
crosses the hill and a Celtic shrine was uncovered near the Roman
temple site.

To reach the temple follow the north rampart until the foundations are seen.

The temple has been described elsewhere (AS pages 134-5) and
the surviving foundations reveal an easterly-facing entrance with an
inner cell 16 feet square. Ley lines pass near the site and phenomena
have been experienced nearby (see SD pages 128-134 for folklore and
other points of interest). The hill was once held as sacred by the Celts
and the name may have derived from the maiden aspect of the triple
goddess Brighid. From a distance the hill appears as a prone figure
stretched out on the landscape. For those who dowse, the hill will be
of interest, particularly the area of the temple.

The remains of the Roman
temple at Maiden Castle.

Two of the ancient barrows beside
the ancient ridgeway track.

✦◇✦◇✦◇✦◇✦◇✦◇✦◇✦◇✦◇✦◇✦◇✦◇✦◇✦

"Here on this height
purity and blessing
comes welling out
of the earth"

(Grace & Ivan Cooke, speaking of the hill in 'The Light in Britain').

✦◇✦◇✦◇✦◇✦◇✦◇✦◇✦◇✦◇✦◇✦◇✦◇✦

Continue along the north rampart and upon reaching the far side pass through the gate, go down the short track and turn right following the well-beaten path to the fingerpost then down the hillside turning right into the lane at the bottom. Follow it round, across a minor junction and up to the road. Turn left and almost immediately take the track on the right towards Higher Ashton Farm, bridleway signposted to Friar Waddon.

Follow the blue waymarked signs ahead, past the farm buildings, through the gates and up the farm road. This well surfaced chalk track rises steadily towards two gates. Pass through the one on the left and go up the field beside the hedge to the gate at the top then bear half right up and across the field passing tumuli on the right making for the gate in the corner. Cross the track maintaining direction towards the fingerpost on the horizon and turn right.

For the next few miles the track passes dozens of Bronze Age barrows, whilst many more are seen on the adjacent hills and on skylines. The important figures buried in them, chiefs and their families, priests and priestesses, were put to rest quite literally half way to the gods on the high ridge. Some of the mounds were astronomically positioned and others would have been visible from surrounding villages, linking the living with their departed ancestors.

Keep to this very scenic inland route of the Dorset Coastal Path, passing between more tumuli then onto a bluebell fringed track and field paths.

After a mile note the large flat boundary stones, mentioned in a Saxon charter dating from 1024 (see AS fig. 107 and plate 86).

Ignore any side turnings until you eventually reach the road at which point turn left and almost immediately join the signed footpath on the right which rises steadily through a small pine bluebell wood. Cross the road and head for the monument. Pass the monument on your left and bear right beside the pit onto the track down the hillside. Further on fork right, cross the track, go down through the bluebell wood and rejoin the track. Fork left to the bottom turning right by the stone farm buildings footpath signed, West Bexington 4½. The little path bears to the left over a stone stile rising beside the field boundary on the left. Part way up cross into the field by the marker stone and make your way up to the Hellstone.

The Hellstone, a Neolithic chambered tomb.

The Hellstone is Dorset's finest surviving Neolithic chambered tomb. Nine large sarsens support an intricately balanced 20 ton cap-

The Head in the stone at the Hellstone, in profile, facing right.

stone. One can enter the interior chamber and step back 6000 years. The chamber was seen as the womb of the Earth Mother, where initiates spent time alone, to be re-birthed. We too can sit in the chamber to rest and perhaps reflect on the pilgrimage thus far. The entrance aligns with the winter solstice sunrise, a key festival date in prehistory when the sun, along with the earth, was thought to be reborn. An important discovery has recently been made at the Hellstone. Researcher and author Terence Meaden recently published new findings in his book 'The Secrets of the Avebury Stones', in which he cites dozens of heads and faces on the huge stones at Avebury, Stonehenge and elsewhere. He sees them as possessing important symbolism to the monument builders, representing perhaps gods and goddesses. A huge head has been found at the Hellstone, on one of the stones on the south side. The well defined eye, nose and mouth face into the chamber and would have been evident when the stone was chosen. Peter Knight has discovered more heads at Rempstone and the Agglestone (see Pilgrimage 10) and other newly discovered examples will be seen later on during this walk, at The Grey Mare and Her Colts. The Hellstone was certainly built with the surrounding landscape and other nearby sites in mind. Ley lines and astronomical alignments have been found associated with the Hellstone (see AS figs. 80 and 82).

❖❖❖❖❖❖❖❖❖❖❖❖❖❖❖❖❖❖❖❖❖❖❖❖❖❖❖❖

How did I not see you, Oh spirit of the stone,
Where you hiding, disguised, did I need to be shown?
You backwardly glance at my sad refrain,
You waited patiently, again and again.
Gazing into the tomb, into our eternity,
How many came this way before there was me?
Did they behold you and think nought of it,
A trick of the light, some weathering grit?
Or have you been glimpsed by others before,
Perhaps those who erected you stood here in awe.
But since then how few have stared into your eye,
Recognising with wonder, and pausing to ask "why?"
(Extract from 'Stone Face' by Peter Knight).

❖❖❖❖❖❖❖❖❖❖❖❖❖❖❖❖❖❖❖❖❖❖❖❖❖❖❖❖

Either retrace your steps or follow the signed path west across the field to the stile in the corner. Keep straight ahead to the stile turning left into the road. Carefully cross over and soon join the track on the right, signed Abbotsbury 2. Pass through the gate and onto the track beyond. Where the path skirts the woods look for a gate giving access to the woods.

Next to the gate, low down to its left in the hedgerow, lie two large stones (often obscured in summer). These once forgotten stones mark not only a ley line heading east to the Hellstone (see AS fig. 82), but also the previously suggested ancient processional route which connects six of the stone sites visited in this pilgrimage (see AS fig. 76).

The Hampton Hill Stone Circle.

Continue up the track, the processional route itself, to the Hampton Hill Stone Circle, on the crest of the hill.

Excavations in 1965 suggested a hollowed way into the circle, with three wooden posts. The circle is small, about 20 feet in diameter made up of about a dozen stones now (more were formerly seen). The views from the site give clues to why the circle was positioned here. To the NE the Hardy Monument marks a hilltop peppered in barrows. From the circle this is where the sun rises at Beltaine (May) and Lammas (August), ancient pre-Christian festivals. Imbolic (February) and Samhain (November 1st) festivals are incredibly marked on the landscape where the cliffs of White Nothe plunge into the sea (see SD fig. 51). Looking west we can see woods on the skyline. These contain barrows which formerly marked out Equinox sunsets when viewed from the circle. At the circle we also stand on a ley line running from the chapel at Abbotsbury to the Hardy Monument (via other sites) and from here we can, unusually, see the entire ley line. We can see St Catherine's Chapel, our pilgrimage destination, for the first time, standing on top of the tor-like hill, which must surely have been sacred in pre-Christian times.

❖❖❖❖❖❖❖❖❖❖❖❖❖❖❖❖❖❖❖❖❖❖❖❖❖❖

These stones speak for themselves: but we must read them
To see what our history could be again,
To stand up and be counted, to renew and mend.
(From 'Sacred Way' by Jay Ramsey).

❖❖❖❖❖❖❖❖❖❖❖❖❖❖❖❖❖❖❖❖❖❖❖❖❖❖

Leaving the stone circle, continue along the track absorbing the magnificent views towards Chesil Beach. Cross the stile and negotiate the hillside path to the marker stone turning right up to the gate, out into the road turning right. Take the next turning on the left pausing where the track divides.

In the hedgerow to the left of the gate to Gorwell Farm lies a large stone (often heavily overgrown in summer). It was formerly the moot stone for the local villages. Prior to this it was probably a megalithic marker of great antiquity marking not only the ancient ridgeway route to the Kingston Russell Stone Circle and other related sites, but also a ley running from this locality all the way to Wool (see AS fig.82).

Take the right fork onto the gravel track and into the field ahead, signposted Kingston Russell Stone Circle. Keep to the bluebell fringed boundary, into a second field and immediately find the stile on the left. Follow the hedge line west round to the gate to visit the Grey Mare and Her Colts Long Barrow.

This long barrow is relatively well preserved, with a fine 75 feet long mound and large megaliths at the SE end (see AS fig. 75 for plan). Like so many other Neolithic long barrows (including the Hellstone we visited earlier) the whole structure is aligned with the summer solstice sunset and the winter solstice sunrise. Note how the barrow is away from the Ridgeway path, on a knoll enabling distant skyline views. Peter Knight has successfully demonstrated, to both 1995 and 1998 field trip parties, how the sun on midsummer day sets betwixt two breast-shaped hills on the skyline (see AS fig.17). In many places around the world the sun rises or sets between similar shaped hills seen from sacred sites, thought to be symbolic of a 'marriage' between the Sky God and the Earth Mother. Another important discovery by Peter Knight in 1999 is of two stone heads on the southern megalith at the barrow, illustrated here. This confirms work by Terence Meaden at Avebury and compliments the head we saw at the Hellstone. The first head has to be viewed from a specific direction standing on the mound and promptly 'disappears' as one moves off line, a feature of most of the Avebury heads. The second head is literally the whole of one side of the same megalith, this time viewed from the SE. The one head clearly shows ram-like horns, inviting connections to the horned deities of the ancient Britons and the Celts, such as Cernunnos. These heads, like the ones at Avebury, Stonehenge and the Hellstone, were part of the rituals once observed at these places. They had been waiting discovery for over 4000 years.

The Grey Mare and her Colts. The stone head is at the left extremity, visible in early afternoon sun.

Return to the stile and continue westward along this mostly dry grass surfaced bridleway, a picture in summer with pink campion, bluebells and white cow parsley carpeting areas beside the hedge.

Approximately 20 yards before the path goes through the hedge gap, note the large stone lying in the ditch on the left. This stone was discovered by Peter Knight in 1994 and is about 6 feet long and roughly triangular. It has been named the Goddess Stone as it is similar in form to many in Brittany, possessing a neck, shoulders and vulva depression (see SD fig. 57). The antiquity of the stone is confirmed by the fact that it lies at the intersection of two leys (see AS figs. 77 and 104, described as the stone at grid ref. 583873).

Continue west and at the far side of the next field go through the hedge gap to the Kingston Russell Stone Circle.

A roughly elliptical circle 90 feet by 80 feet is formed by 18 prone stones. Some may not be in their original position and there are gaps in the circle. Dowsers have detected earth energies spiralling around the circle before leaving to travel across the landscape. Some astronomical alignments have been found associated with the circle (AS Fig. 87) and two leys intersect here (AS figs. 77 and 88). The circle offers commanding views of The Knoll to the west and Abbotsbury Ridge to the south.

The Grey Mare and Her Colts looking SE. Low down to the right is the second head; the horn is only visible around mid-afternoon.

Return to the path, go through the gate in the corner and stay on the field path beside the hedge, down through the gates to the track at the bottom. Turn left, through Gorwell Farm following the drive to the end of the wood then take the concrete

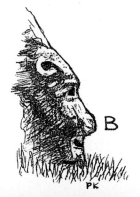

The two heads at the Grey Mare and Her Colts. A: view from SE. B: view from NW. Sun in south. (features vary with direction of sun.)

drive leading to the gate on the right. Climb the track to the gate at the top and keep straight ahead down the field to the gate at the bottom, a magnificent viewpoint. Bear right past the tumuli, down the hillside to the metal gate, across the field to a similar gate and left down the sunken track. Further on beyond the gate an attractive path drops gently to the village of Abbotsbury. At the road turn right then next left, following signs to the Abbey and Abbey Barn.

On the left side of the lane, west of the church tower, sits a 4 foot long ley markstone, associated with a ley going from the chapel on the hill to the Hampton Hill Stone Circle, visited earlier (see AS fig. 70 and plate 53).

Go through the old arch of the abbey nearby.

Little remains now of the abbey founded in 1044 by Orc, steward to King Canute. Some walls still stand and by the path near the church lie some fragments of worked stone. The foundation was a Benedictine monastery and stood for 500 years until the Dissolution. Outside the church of St Nicholas, next to the wall on the south side, are the remains of a medieval stone cross, with its octagonal base and a small shaft stump (see AS plate 52). Inside the church is an exceptional stained glass window of St Catherine, a work of great beauty.

Continue down the lane to the pond and the Abbey Barn.

Huge in its dimensions, 91 yards long, 31 feet high and solidly buttressed, it dates from around 1400 and has stood the test of time incredibly well.

The Abbey Barn and pond at Abbotsbury.

Looking up Chapel Hill at Abbotsbury.

Past the pond take the right fork to the foot of Chapel Hill. A variety of paths lead to the top. One goes steeply up straight ahead or a more gradual route goes right before climbing up the spine of the hill.

As you climb it is worth dwelling on the fact that this tor was probably a sacred place long before the coming of Christianity. Its belly or breast-shape reminds us of Glastonbury Tor which is similarly capped by a chapel to Christianise a locality of great antiquity. St Catherine's Chapel was built in 1370 and was constructed to withstand buffeting by gales. Its walls are 4 feet thick, standing solid against the elements. The old legend tells of how St Catherine was arrested by the Romans in 307 AD, who killed her for not renouncing her Christian faith. After her death she was taken to Mount Sinai by angels, hence her association with hilltops. Chapels at Cerne Abbas, Milton Abbas and St Aldhelm's Head were likewise dedicated. Note the 'wishing holes' on the south doorway into which local girls would drop pins whilst reciting charms to obtain a husband. St Catherine probably replaced a previous female deity that was worshipped at the hill. Old pagan goddesses became female saints as Christianity attempted to overtake sacred sites. Rodney Castleden, in 'The Cerne Giant', makes the same assumption about the Cerne Well, which has a Catherine wheel in stone at the well (see Pilgrimage 4). The hill is linked to prehistoric ritual by a ley line that runs from the chapel to the Hardy monument (with its adjacent tumuli) via the Hampton Hill Stone Circle (see AS fig. 70). Also, to the north west, the ramparts of the prehistoric Abbotsbury Castle hill fort can be seen. The earthworks contain Bronze Age tumuli indicating an ancient sacred place. From the chapel the summer solstice sun sets into the hill fort. The distant views, elevated height and chapel all come together to create a place of great sanctity, a fitting place to end this pilgrimage. For thousands of years Man has been climbing to the top of hills such as this, hills deemed holy, where one is quite literally 'halfway to the Gods'.

The Chapel at Abbotsbury, seen from the Abbey arch.

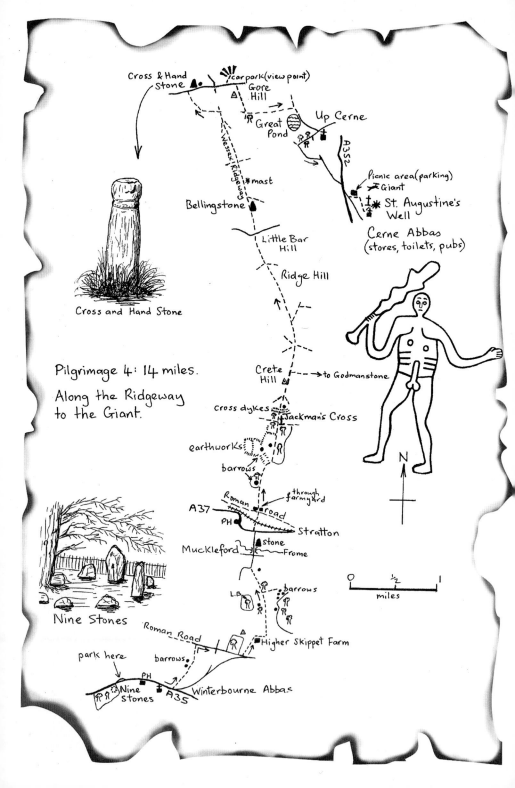

Cross & Hand Stone

car park (view point)

Gore Hill

Up Cerne

Great Pond

A352

Wessex Ridgeway

*mast

Bellingstone

Cross and Hand Stone

Picnic area (parking)
Giant
St. Augustine's Well

Cerne Abbas
(stores, toilets, pubs)

Little Bar Hill

Ridge Hill

Pilgrimage 4: 14 miles.
Along the Ridgeway
to the Giant.

Crete Hill ────→ to Godmanstone

cross dykes
Jackman's Cross

earthworks

barrows

N

through farmyard

Roman road
A37
PH ──── Stratton

Muckleford ── stone
Frome

L.B. ─ barrows

Nine Stones

Roman Road

Higher Skippet Farm

park here
barrows
PH
Nine Stones ── A35 ── Winterbourne Abbas

0   ½   1
miles

ALONG THE RIDGEWAY TO THE GIANT

An uplifting pilgrimage along an ancient ridgeway route, beginning and passing prehistoric sacred places, ending at Cerne's Giant and holy spring. A synthesis of beautiful scenery and tranquil paths. The route is not too strenuous, with only a couple of moderate climbs. Wild hedgerow flowers and woods carpeted in bluebells, compliment this pilgrimage. Refreshment is limited on route. There is a pub at the start and another in Grimstone requiring a short diversion along the A37, otherwise nothing until you reach Cerne Abbas.

Start: Nine Stones Stone Circle, on A35, west of Winterbourne Abbas.

OS Maps: Landranger 194 and Explorer 117.
Reference: 612/904.

Approximate distance: 14 miles. Godmanstone is convenient for a split walk. It is reached via a public footpath from Crete Hill (see map).

This pilgrimage begins at the Nine Stones, one of the finest Bronze Age stone circles in the south but unfortunately plagued by its close proximity to the busy A35. The nearest parking is at a small lay-by at the barn to the NE. Great care should be taken in not blocking the farm entrance and when crossing the fast road.

❖❖❖❖❖❖❖❖❖❖❖❖❖❖❖❖❖❖❖❖❖❖❖❖❖

Nine Men a-dancing 'neath the tall trees,
Under Grandmother Beech, Pan's pipes fill the breeze,
You circle about me, I join in your jig,
As you dance around, playing catch and tig.
You spin and weave and embrace at life's thrill,
But quick, someone's coming! Back to sleep, stony still.
'Nine Stones Ode', by Peter Knight.

❖❖❖❖❖❖❖❖❖❖❖❖❖❖❖❖❖❖❖❖❖❖❖❖❖

The Nine Stones, nestling beneath its guardian beech.

67

A large beech overshadows and indeed guards the ancient stones and in fact undeniably adds to the mystic atmosphere of the place. The nine megaliths form an ellipse, facilitating astronomical alignments. The tallest stone is not only phallic-shaped but also has two symbolic vulva-shaped holes, used for votive offerings, both in ancient times and today. The stone is noteworthy in combining male-god and earth goddess symbolism.

Looking at this tallest stone from the direction of the gate the profile of a head can be made out on the left side of the stone. This may not be by chance. Work by Terence Meaden ('The Secrets of the Avebury Stones') has revealed dozens of left-facing heads in the stones at Avebury and elsewhere. They may well have formed the backdrop to the rituals. We will see other faces in stone on our pilgrimages at Rempstone, the Hellstone and the Agglestone.

Several astronomical alignments have been demonstrated previously (see AS fig. 102 and SD fig. 50). The most easily demonstrated is the Beltaine/Lammas sunrise (early May and early August) which is aligned with barrows on the skyline looking east from the circle (look for the isolated trees on them). These are on Pound Hill and we will in fact walk past them later on this pilgrimage (see AS fig. 16 for the view in question).

left: The symbolic vulvar hole at the base of the tallest megalith of the Nine Stones.

right: The left-facing profile of the tallest Nine Stones megalith. The arrow marks the eye. (Photo by Terence Meaden)

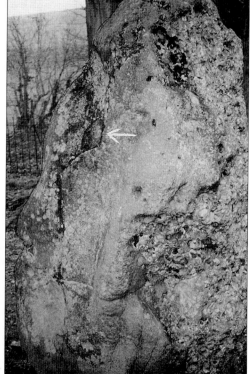

Modern pilgrims walking down the Roman road north of Winterbourne Abbas.

Leave the sanctity of the Nine Stones and proceed east along the very fast A35 keeping to the safer north side of the road. Walk through Winterbourne Abbas and take the path north immediately west of the petrol station. Continue upwards and northwards over stiles until we pass the Bronze Age barrows we saw so strategically placed to be visible from the Nine Stones. To view them look for a break in the hedge near a clump of five trees. The path comes out at a Roman road which heads straight in to Dorchester. Walk east down hill, admiring the bluebells and pink campion in spring. Just before the A35 take the path north signposted, Bradford Peverell 2¼, climbing upwards to open ground with clear distant views. Join the farm track into Higher Skippet Farm. Just east of the farm take the bridleway north into quieter realms, leaving at last the rumble of the A35 behind. Just before reaching the overhead power lines look to the left and note a lovely Bronze Age barrow at the edge of the small wood. The more distant wood hides a much older Neolithic long barrow. Ignore the path on the right and enjoy banks full of cowslips encountered, accompanied by chaffinches and hawks overhead. On rejoining the tarmac road turn right to the bridge at Muckleford.

Here the Frome meanders across the valley floor, flowing eternally down to the sea at Wareham. Immediately north of the bridge, on the east side of the road, is the Muckleford Markstone. This was discovered by Peter Knight only a few years ago and is in fact the lonely sentinel at the intersection of two ley alignments, one going all the way to Stonehenge (see AS figs. 13 and 104). Few passing it today would realise the sanctity and antiquity of this isolated wayside stone. Its large flat surface invites the pilgrim to rest at this tranquil spot on the ley to the 'Temple on the Plain'.

Continue north soon to reach the busy A37. Carefully cross to the signposted bridleway opposite and walk north again, crossing the railway, then another Roman track and on through the farm. We are now walking along one of the ancient ridgeways, first trod by our prehistoric ancestors. Another round barrow can soon be seen in the woods on your left before the path skirts around the reservoir. Walk through the gate and you are in an area of ancient habitation and burial. Earthworks of prehistoric and Iron Age settlements can be seen west of the path along with a couple of barrows. We now encounter a small clearing in the woods.

The stump of Jackman's Cross can be found to the east of the intersecting paths, dating from medieval times with a cup-shaped alms cavity (see AS for ley connections and folklore).

Continue along the ridgeway past cross dykes and a barrow. Beyond the gate the land opens with distant views west, but short lived as we then enter a section hemmed in by hedgerows. Pass through the next gate ignoring all side paths. There are uplifting views as we skirt the sides of Ridge Hill and Little Bar Hill before reaching the road. Cross over and continue north on to the bridleway which climbs gently to the Bellingstone, located in the hedgerow on the north side of the track as the hill levels out.

The Muckleford Stone next to the Frome.

This large megalith is aligned with the Cerne Giant, about a mile to the north-east. Hedgerows and trees now prevent what was once a visible alignment. Around May Day, the old fertility festival of Beltaine, the sun would rise over the Giant when viewed from the stone. This certainly links in with the phallic symbolism of the Giant. The stone is smooth on the east side yet pot-marked with cavities on the track side. The larger holes may have been used for votive offerings, a common practice at ancient and Classical sites. Just north of the Bellingstone a gap in the hedgerow enables a view of the proud Giant, with club in hand. Although we are further away from the Giant than the viewing lay-by on the A352, he is not so foreshortened from here.

❖❖❖❖❖❖❖❖❖❖❖❖❖❖❖❖❖❖❖❖❖❖❖❖

'Here come I, Beelzebub,
And over my shoulders
I carry a club'
(Christmas Mummers' play).

❖❖❖❖❖❖❖❖❖❖❖❖❖❖❖❖❖❖❖❖❖❖❖❖

Looking back along the ancient ridgeway track from the Bellingstone.

Walk past the tower and enjoy the peace of this stretch of the ridgeway path with its bluebell woods and banks of campion, stitchwort and bluebells. At grid ref: 637033 is an intersection of paths where the Wessex Ridgeway bears right. The path ahead is often difficult to traverse so turn left skirting Redpost Hill which plunges to Eastcombe Bottom. Upon reaching the road turn right soon encountering the Cross and Hand Stone on the left-hand verge.

The Bellingstone, ancient ridgeway sentinel linked with the Cerne Abbas.

(See drawing on Pilgrimage 4 map and AS plate 104). The views north from the stone are wonderful, with the Mendips, Glastonbury Tor and Devon hills in the distance. The stone itself is noticeably phallic-shaped, of unknown age and steeped in legend (see Chapter Two, 'Miracles? Walk This Way' and AS pages 22 –25 for folklore). This stone is unique in the south but similar shaped ones occur in Scotland, Cheshire and in Africa. The locality was clearly a place of great significance in the past, and is certainly still one of mystery today. Four round barrows, now levelled, once stood in the field north of the stone.

Walk east along the road, ignoring the plunging road on the left. The picnic view point on the left affords more brilliant distant vistas. Back on the road continue east for a short stretch and take the footpath south which passes east of the trig. point across open ground heading for a clump of trees, then turn left along Wether Hill. Views to the south show how Up Cerne nestles in a bowl in the chalk downlands, the Manor House and church standing out. At the end of the east-west path turn right descending past the Great Pond then right at the junction. The Manor grounds are on the left as we walk down an avenue of trees. Look left and one can glimpse the Cerne Giant, now less than a mile away. Keep on the road as it turns south to meet the A352 turning right to the viewing point.

❖-❖

Oh man of the hill, wealder of mighty club,
Are you Hercules, Helith or Beelzebub?
Do you raise your club in anger, or out of neglect,
Or in silent salute for the Earth you respect?
With proud member you fertilise the land, our Mother,
Remembering times past, Earth Goddess, no other.
You are man of mysteries and of Truth,
And hope to many a childless lass and youth.
You gaze across the vale, eternities role by,
Oh Man of Cerne, I am a twinkling of your eye.
"Silent Salute", by Peter Knight, spring 1999

❖-❖

Controversy still rages as to the purpose and age of the Giant, and these issues are discussed at length elsewhere (see SD pages 78 – 79 and 'The Cerne Giant' by Rodney Casleden, the definitive guide to the prehistory of the Cerne area). He stands 55 metres high, unashamedly displaying his 7 metre long phallus. The hill above is rich in sacred places, such as barrows, enclosures and a Celtic shrine enclosed in the Trendle, the earthworks visible on the skyline from the lay-by. The whole area around Cerne was once sacred ground where the local Durotriges tribe gathered for festivals and rituals revolving around the turning year.

The beautiful walk by the river as the pilgrimage route approaches Cerne Abbas.

Walk now south, taking the left fork off the main road descending until a track going west is encountered (marked 'picnic area' and 'pottery'). Just past the picnic area take the footpath right, which follows the River Cerne south into the village. The walk here is shaded with the river gently ambling alongside. On reaching a white cottage take the footbridge over the river and follow the enclosed path to the duck pond. This pond is in fact fed by the spring that is our destination, but for the moment we turn right, taking the short walk down the lane to the church.

St Mary's was built in 1260, the chancel being the oldest surviving part, whilst the tower dates from 1500 –1520. A fascinating collection of gargoyles and other strange carvings adorn the church's exterior. One is a face-puller, another creature is eating a baby, with others showing men wielding clubs and axes, referring perhaps to the Giant nearby. One with a huge gaping mouth (illustrated here) was used in the past as a smoke flue. The images are overtly pre-Christian,

Wide-mouthed carving on the outside of St Mary's, Cerne Abbas.

symbols of the old pagan days utilised for warding off evil spirits, what ever they might be! The area was strongly pagan long after Christianity spread across Dorset. A local record as late as 1250 speaks of locals worshipping the sun god Helis or Helith.

Walk back to the duck pond and just past it go through an arched gate into the abbey churchyard.

On the wall to your right is a plaque telling of the interesting folk-lore of the well, and the curative properties of the waters. But we will take a brief diversion before going to the sacred well by following the path going north across the graveyard. On your right you will see the remains of a medieval preaching cross, with its broken off shaft (see AS plate 100). Go through another arched gate out into open ground. On the wall on the right is a plaque commemorating a pilgrimage by the faithful in August 1987 to celebrate the 1000th anniversary of the founding of Cerne Abbey, in the late 10th century. The Benedictines came here to Christianise what was already a sacred place. Broken ground in the field towards Giant Hill probably testifies to a pre-Christian 'sanctuary', according to Rodney Castleden. The area certainly lies in alignment with the well and the Trendle shrine.

Going back into the churchyard head for the east corner of the grounds, where the well is located. Access is via a stony path shaded by large lime trees.

The atmosphere is one of timeless sanctity, a fitting destination for our pilgrimage. The water in fact flows from a natural spring and the waters have been seen since ancient times as flowing from the womb of the Earth Goddess. Many curative traditions are associated with the locality and one can see why the abbey was literally built around it. It has been demonstrated previously (AS fig.13) how a ley alignment going from Holwell to Winterbourne Steepleton passes straight through the abbey site and a link has also been suggested between curative wells and springs and some leys that cross Dorset (see SD Chapter 6).

As one sits in contemplation at this ancient sacred site, perhaps we can look back over this pilgrimage, with its discoveries and experiences, and reflect on the countless pilgrims who have come here before. For at this place and time you are linked to them all.

The well at Cerne Abbas. The arrow points to the wishing stone with its Catherine Wheel. This symbol is an ancient symbol denoting the eight festivals of the solar year.

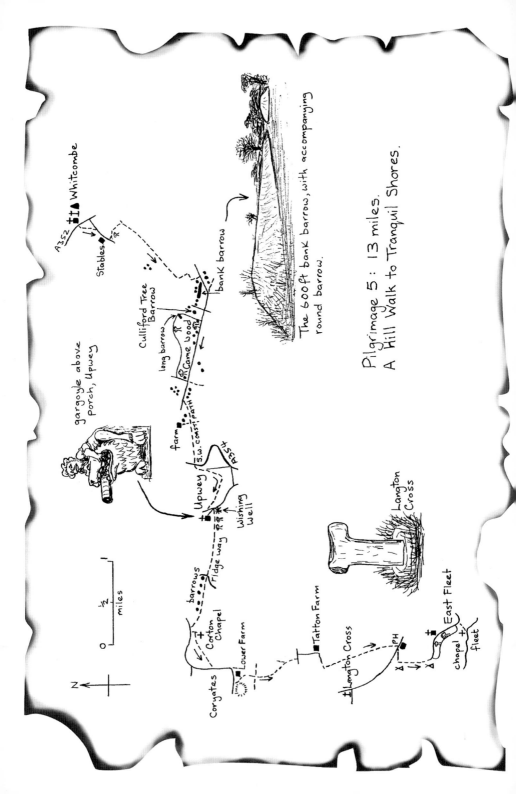

The 600ft bank barrow, with accompanying round barrow.

Pilgrimage 5 : 13 miles.
A Hill Walk to Tranquil Shores.

Whitcombe

A352

Stables

bank barrow

Culliford Tree Barrow

long barrow

Came Wood

farm

S.W. COAST PATH

gargoyle above porch, Upwey

Upwey

A354

Wishing Well

Ridge way

barrows

Corton Chapel

Coryates

Lower Farm

Tatton Farm

Langton Cross

Langton Cross

Langton Cross

PH

East Fleet

chapel

Fleet

N

0   ½   miles

A HILL WALK TO TRANQUIL WATERS

Start at Whitcombe. Village located on the A352 south of Dorchester. There is small lay-by opposite church.

OS Maps: Landranger 194 and Outdoor Leisure 15. Reference: 717/882.

Approximate distance: 13 miles. Elwell or Upwey, which are just off the A354 are ideal spots for a split walk.

Steep in places and a little demanding this very enjoyable walk in the main follows old bridleway tracks and field paths. The going is generally good underfoot but expect some muddy areas near the farms in winter. There is a good pub in Elwel, a tea room at Upwey and a pub near the end.

Whitcombe Church dates from around the 10th century and was part of the original endowment of Milton Abbey by King Athelstan. However the site was used prior to this as a sacred place. Look for the stone around which the wall has been built to the right of the churchyard gate (arrowed in photo). This may have been a ley marker-stone, standing originally on an alignment going from Mount Pleasant Henge to Broadmayne (see AS fig. 91 and plate 94). Near the porch stands the socket stone and shaft of a 14th – 15th century stone

Whitcombe Church. The arrow marks an older stone.

Two crosses, fragments of Saxon age in Whitcombe Church.

Whitcombe Church, with 13th century font in foreground. The serenity of the church is unavoidable.

cross. At the east end of the church, on the exterior window arch stop, two weathered carved heads can be found. One is horned with an open mouth, a typical 'frightener' of church architecture, yet echoing previous pagan symbolism. Moving into the church, much of the stonework is Saxon and Norman. Immediately opposite the door rest two fragments of a Saxon cross. To the right of these is a faded late-14th century wall painting showing St Christopher carrying the Christ Child across a river. To the right of him a mermaid raises herself from the waters. The font at the west end is 13th century. The church certainly has an air of peacefulness and sacredness, a fitting beginning to the pilgrimage.

After visiting the church carefully cross this busy road and join the footpath, signposted to Whitcombe Barn, which heads half left across fields to a narrow lane. Turn right walking until you reach a signed bridleway on the left then keep to this gently rising grass and stone track, over the horse ride walking until you eventually reach a cross bridleway then turn right. This lovely track, often wet in winter and overgrown in summer, is very peaceful, surrounded by fields and home to many native butterflies. Walk to the end of the track at which point turn left through the hedge gap and follow the field path up beside the boundary and all the way round the top before reaching the

The Neolithic bank barrow, east of Came Wood.

The wishing well at Upwey, an ancient sacred locality.

gates allowing access to the lane. Turn right keeping to the right-hand side.

Note the large Bronze Age barrows soon encountered on either side of the lane. In the field to the west a much longer mound will be seen. This 600 foot long bank barrow is of Neolithic Age, some 5000 - 6000 years old. It is purposefully aligned with the northernmost rising of the moon in summer, which is also almost coincidental to where the sun rises on Samhain and Imbolc festivals, in early November and February respectively. Note the Bronze Age tumuli around the much older bank barrow, indicating a sacred place revered over hundreds of years. For the next mile westwards note how the elevated land was utilised by Bronze Age man, with the building of numerous round barrows. Some of the local mounds have mysterious folklore (see SD).

Walk past Came Wood, noting good views of Portland, Chalbury Hill Fort and more tumuli on the skyline on Bincombe Hill to the south. A short distance up the hill on the left join the signposted Inland Coastal Path. Follow the fence line up to the gate, cross the track to the gate opposite forking right onto the grass track that rises to a gate and wide track beyond. Further on go through the gate on the right and negotiate the narrow path through more gates leading down to the road. Carefully cross to the stile opposite, over the field to the stile in the hedge turning left onto this rather uneven track which descends gently towards Elwell. Just before reaching the Ship Inn, a very good refreshment stop, look for the short track on the right and follow it behind the dwellings up to the stile. Carry on to the next stile and along the field boundary to another stile eventually arriving in the rear garden of a large house. Keep straight ahead to the stone stile and along the driveway turning left into the lane and then right to visit Upwey church.

West of Upwey the track ascends, skirting woodland, with views north to the Ridgeway.

St Bartholomew, Corton.

The church of St Lawrence as we see it today dates from the 13 – 14th century with later refinements. This replaced an early wooden chapel and a later chantry dated 1243. The siting of the church is due to the nearby well, which has always been a healing and pilgrimage destination. To the left of the porch note the gargoyle in the form of 'a boy holding open a wolf's mouth' according to the church guide-book. However, a flower-like head-dress and triangular eyes make the figure more otherworldly than human. The 'wolf' in fact has rounded not sharp teeth and appears more mystic in nature. Around the other side of the church, on the south side, three fine demonic-looking gargoyles are low down on the stonework for easy inspection. One enters the church by opening a 500-year-old, iron-studded oak and elm door. On the nearest pillar to the tower is a fine carving of the Green Man, a pre-Christian icon representing the fertility and life-force of nature. Only a handful are known in Dorset (see Pilgrimage 2, Evershot church for others). Other interesting features inside include the medieval font, wall paintings and old window glass.

Return down the lane to the Wishing Well. Opening times usually from Easter to mid-December, but sometimes closed Monday and Tuesday. Telephone: 01305 814470. There is an excellent tea garden and café on site.

The well and its gardens are one of Dorset's treasures, a place of shady paths and trickling waters. The well is in fact a spring, the

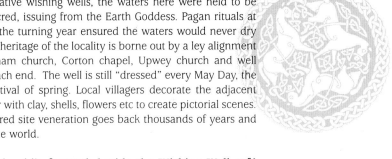

source of the Wey and one of the most powerful in the country. Water issues from below at a rate of up to 1½ million gallons a day. Like so many other curative wishing wells, the waters here were held to be magical and sacred, issuing from the Earth Goddess. Pagan rituals at key festivals of the turning year ensured the waters would never dry up. The ancient heritage of the locality is borne out by a ley alignment through Portesham church, Corton chapel, Upwey church and well and tumuli at each end. The well is still "dressed" every May Day, the old Beltaine festival of spring. Local villagers decorate the adjacent Victorian shelter with clay, shells, flowers etc to create pictorial scenes. This type of sacred site veneration goes back thousands of years and occurs across the world.

Join the signed public footpath beside the Wishing Well café and follow the track up to the stile, beyond which it rises very steeply to a stile near the top. Keeping close to the hedge walk to the gate on the far side of the field maintaining direction along Friar Waddon Hill. At the stile cross the metalled track and head between the tumuli towards the pylons, across the hill, down to the stile and into the road turning left. Almost immediately turn left down the concrete road and join the signed footpath on the right, which leads to the little church at Corton Farm. There is a stile behind the church.

Corton is a cluster of farm buildings and cottages built of beautiful Portland and Purbeck stone, with old beams to add further character. The views south to Portland are uplifting. The small chapel appears balanced on a steep scarp and the natural local stone blends perfectly with the locality. A chapel was here possibly as early as the 4th century. Most of the present building is 13th century with later renovations. Inside is a rare example of a pre-Reformation stone altar, probably hidden by Catholics in 1550, following an order by Edward VI that "all altar stones used for Catholic mass should be destroyed". It is of local Purbeck stone. It has already been mentioned how this chapel lies on a ley line, which connects it with Upwey church and well. Some surviving evidence for this could be a large stone, on which the chapel rests, to the left of the door. Many other Dorset churches have been found to possess ancient stones in their fabric or else close by (see Whitcombe, Cattistock, Knowlton, Abbotsbury and Melbury Abbas, all in this guide)

Continue the walk heading away from the church and up the hillside to the corner of the fenced field (path not very well defined). Stay close to the fence and further on pick a route down the hillside making for the stone bridge and stile. Turn left heading down the hill through Coryates. Corfe Gates House is a highly commended bed & breakfast establishment. Turn right at the bend and carry on past the farm buildings

until you come to the stile on the left. Cross to the stiles and bridge opposite then bear left and make for the stile in the top corner. Walk up beside the hedge round the fenced area to the stile then go slightly left up the field to the stile at the top. Bearing left walk down the field to the gap in the hedge, pass through and make your way left across the field to the stile in the far corner. Cross another stile and maintain direction to the top left hand corner, though the gap to the stile bearing left round the edge of the field to the gate. Follow the hedge line down to the stile, stream and bridge and go straight up the field to the stile at the top turning left into the road.

Walk for just a short distance then take the turning on the right to Tatton Farm, bearing right at the entrance to the field then left. Ignore the gate and stile on the right but continue walking until you reach a gate leading to the field ahead. Go up the rise to the stiles in the top corner then down the field heading towards the Victoria Inn where a stile allows access to the road. On the right-hand side of the pub is a signed footpath. Keeping to the right-hand side of the hedge walk to the top of the field and turn left on the drive leading down to the holiday centre and straight ahead up the old coach track, finally turning left into the road following it all the way to Fleet.

The rare Pre-Reformation altar at Corton.

The tiny chapel at East Fleet.

The parish church of the Holy Trinity was built between 1827-29 in the Gothic style. Inside, on the south wall of the tower, a marble tablet records the destruction of the old church by a severe storm in 1824.

Continue south along the lane and at the sharp bend turn right, walking past the cottages to the old church.

Only part of the old church now remains, the rest having been destroyed by the 1824 gale. The small chancel now survives as a mortuary chapel. In 1827 a new west wall was built, but the remainder is original. The tiny building is dwarfed by tall pines and the place is peaceful. A short walk south brings one to the shores of the Fleet with the huge bank of Chesil Beach beyond. Although three miles from the entrance to the sea at Small Mouth there are still high and low tides and the waters are brackish. On calm days the waters are almost rippleless, a tranquil place to end our pilgrimage.

❖❖❖❖❖❖❖❖❖❖❖❖❖❖❖❖❖❖❖❖❖❖❖❖❖❖

"If nature is your teacher, your soul will awaken."
(From Goethe's, "Faust")

❖❖❖❖❖❖❖❖❖❖❖❖❖❖❖❖❖❖❖❖❖❖❖❖❖❖

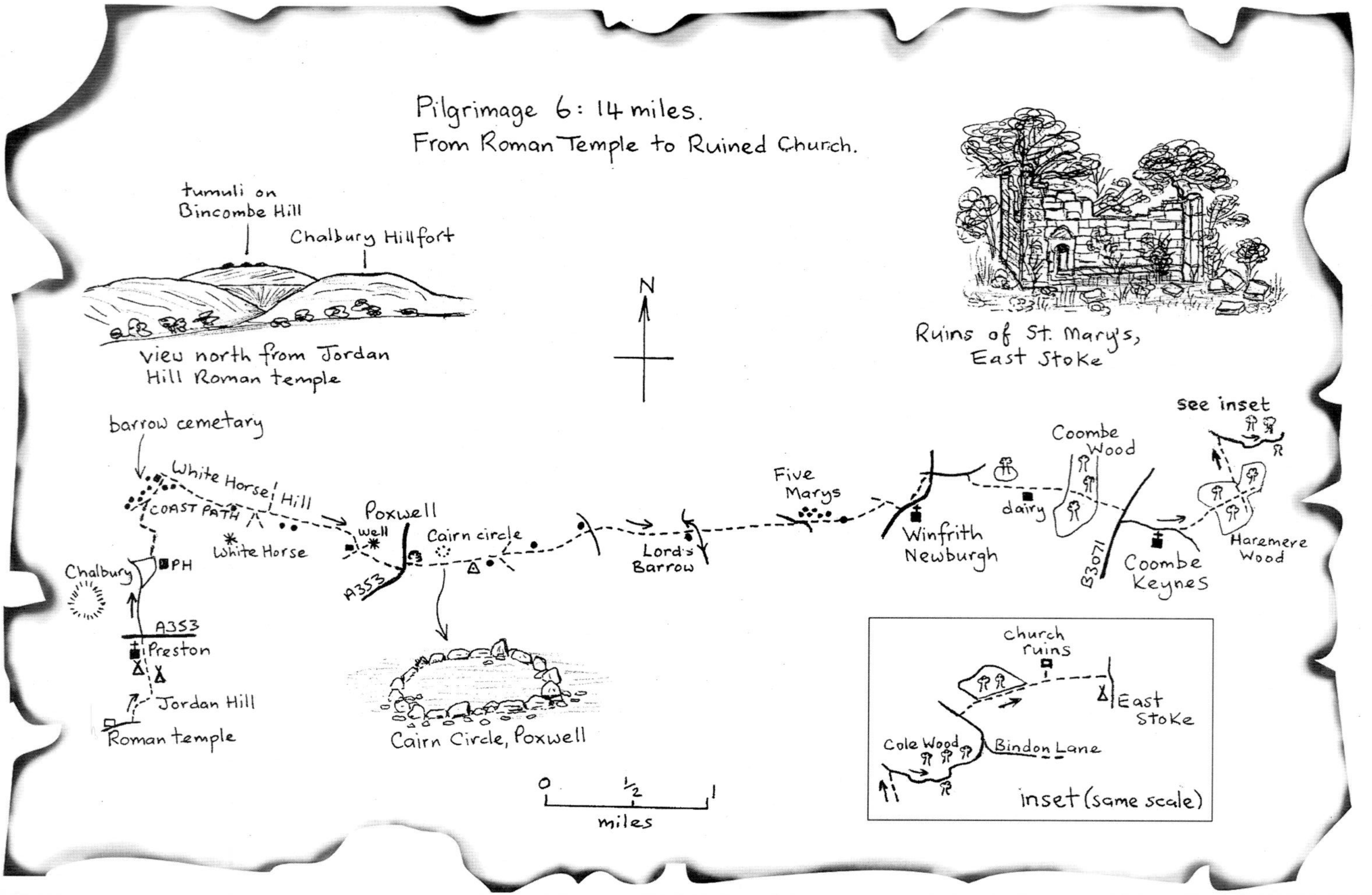

Pilgrimage 6: 14 miles.
From Roman Temple to Ruined Church.

N

Ruins of St. Mary's, East Stoke

see inset

Haremere Wood

Coombe Keynes

B30??

Coombe Wood

dairy

Winfrith Newburgh

Five Marys

Lord's Barrow

tumuli on Bincombe Hill

Chalbury Hillfort

view north from Jordan Hill Roman temple

barrow cemetery

White Horse Hill

COAST PATH

White Horse

Poxwell

well

A353

Cairn circle

Cairn Circle, Poxwell

Chalbury

PH

A353

Preston

Jordan Hill Roman temple

Inset (same scale)

Church ruins

East Stoke

Bindon Lane

Cole Wood

0   ½   1
miles

FROM ROMAN TEMPLE TO RUINED CHURCH

Start from Bowleaze Cove. Take the turning off the A353 up Furzy Cliff and park in the road close to the Roman Temple marker stone. For those interested in public transport there is an hourly train service from Wool to Weymouth. It makes the route slightly longer but gives one the opportunity to see the town and walk beside, or through Lodmoor Country Park. Times vary.

A lengthy but extremely enjoyable walk which first guides you along fairly strenuous, scenic down land bridleways leading to lovely Winfrith Newburgh, followed later by very attractive paths through pretty bluebell woods and passing through the delightful hamlet of Coombe Keynes. Although some areas can be muddy in winter the going is generally good underfoot. There is a pub at Sutton Poyntz overlooking the millpond and a village shop in Winfrith Newburgh, otherwise there are no refreshments on route.

OS Maps: Landranger 194 & Outdoor Leisure 15. Reference: 699/820.

T he foundations of this Romano-British temple of the 3-4th century AD are some 24 feet square, with 3 - 4 feet thick walls. At the SE corner of the site was discovered a 14foot shaft, lined with clay and stone, filled in with many layers of clay containing swords, coins, ashes and other votive offerings. The siting of the temple affords magnificent views. To the north one can see Chalbury Hillfort and to its left tumuli stand on top of Bincombe Hill (see AS Fig. 56). The intervisibility of these distant ancient sites and its high location may point to use of the locality prior to the arrival of the Romans.

Approximate distance: 14 miles. The lane next to Lord's Barrow offers a split option, approximately half way along the pilgrimage.

Jordon Hill, Roman Temple.

The slaying of the dragon at Preston Church.

The Poxwell Cairn, from the west.

After visiting the temple head east down the hill between the holiday parks taking the next turning on the left, public footpath signed. Keep to the main drive through the holiday park turning left before reaching the service block. Leave by the gate and follow the tarred track to St Andrew's Church Preston.

Probably dating back to the end of the 14th century the church is built in the Gothic style. Note the weathered carving of St Michael or St George slaying a dragon beneath to the east of the porch. Inside the church is a stained glass window in the north wall of particular interest to those on the pilgrimage. It illustrates Bunyan's 'Pilgrims Progress'. The church font is Norman and the remains of an 11th century stone cross sits on the SW window ledge, near the organ. The accompanying plaque suggests it came from an 'ancient burial mound' in the vicinity.

Back outside the church, note the two prominent hills to the north, which our ancestors may have regarded as the breasts of the Earth Goddess (see SD Fig.66). Another example of hill symbolism can be found on Pilgrimage 3, at the Grey Mare long Barrow.

Continue up to the main road, carefully cross over in to Sutton Road forking right in the village. After passing the millpond and the Springhead pub, turn left and immediately right onto the narrow track leading to the gate. Keep to this limestone path gently up the hillside, through a couple of gates and then turn left onto the well trodden footpath. Expect to see several butterflies including a number of marbled whites. It is a steep

climb to the top but amply rewarded with good views across Weymouth Bay. Turn right by the gate and carry on along the ridge, through the gate, past the derelict buildings and turn right onto the track. Further on fork right joining the inland route of The Dorset Coast Path signposted, Osmington 1½.

Pass through the gate into the field and carry on to the gate opposite then fork left towards Poxwell. Go through the gate opposite, along the fenced track and through a couple of gates. Further on there is a field on the left; the depression in the middle is the site of a Romano-British grain pit. At the bottom of the field, beside the access point off the track from the village of Poxwell and surrounded by sheep fencing, is Pokes Well which is mentioned in The Domes Day Book.

The name means 'Fairy Well' and many wells across Britain are associated with the 'little people' of folklore. (See SD chapter 3 for more Dorset fairy sites and tales).

Leave by the gate and walk up the rise to the gate ahead, path signed to Holworth. Keep straight ahead across the field then down the gully to the road. Carefully cross over turning left and almost immediately join the bridleway signposted, Holworth 1. Climb gently up this rather uneven and sometimes muddy track.

Poxwell Cairn Circle can be reached a short way up the track by leaving the track and heading north over the ridge. (Grid ref. 744836). The circle is in fact not a true stone circle at all, but the inner stone lining of a round barrow, the mound of which has long since eroded, leaving only the stones. Over 20 stones inscribe a circle 14feet in diameter. Cremation remains found here suggest a date of around 1500 BC, typical of most round barrows, or tumuli. Look for outlying stones to the west and SW of the circle, possibly representing outer mound stones or, as Charles Warne suggested in 1872, an avenue of stones (see AS Fig.52 for site plan).

Charle's Warne's 1872 veiw of Poxwell Cairn, showing the barrow mound and some of the outlying stones.

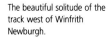

Back on the track continue east along a route not very well defined. Try to maintain your direction across the fields to a gate then bear left down the hillside to another gate and continue along the ridge down to yet another gate. Bearing left continue up the hillside making for the gate in the hedge at the top, through a couple more gates before reaching the road. Cross to the gate opposite and follow this bridleway, (can become overgrown in summer), down through more gates and up to the road beside Lord's Barrow.

The mound rises to about 7 feet and lies around 400 feet above sea level on the crest of a ridge. This Bronze Age epitaph marks the boundaries of Owermoigne and Chaldon Herring. The barrow seems much damaged by excavations.

Cross the lane, through yet more gates until you reach the road then keep straight ahead and shortly join the bridleway, signed Five Mary's and Winfrith. Stay on this scenic path and you will soon encounter the Five Marys group of barrows.

The beautiful solitude of the track west of Winfrith Newburgh.

This sacred place is situated on the spine of an east-west ridge, some 325 feet above sea level. There are in fact six barrows in almost a straight line. They appear as 'Five Meers' on a 1765 map. This may derive from the Anglo-Saxon word 'gemaer' meaning 'boundary', indicating former territorial markers. The barrows were excavated prior to 1866 and revealed some interesting finds of a ritualistic

Coombe Keynes, with thatched cottages and village green shaded by an oak.

Coombe Keynes church.

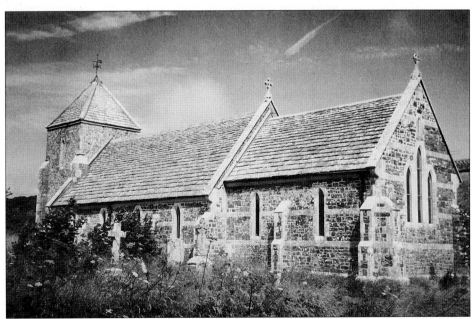

nature. Two of the mounds yielded two male and one female skeletons in the contracted or 'sitting' position and, unusually, all three had antlers on each of their shoulders. The stag features prominently in Celtic and Saxon mythology, a creature representing fertility, the power of nature, death and rebirth. The Celtic god Cernunnos had antlers on his head. Perhaps these three Bronze Age people were actual priests or priestesses, for this type of burial, though not unique, is unusual.

Continue along the track, past another barrow before going downhill, entering Winfrith Newburgh close to the church.

The church is dedicated to St Christopher, patron saint of travellers, making it an apt stop for the millennial pilgrim. The tower is 15th century complete with twelve interesting gargoyles. After entering the church via the very ornate Norman doorway one can look for the surviving 12-13th century wall of the chancel, at the east end of the church. St Christopher can be seen in a stained glass window in the north aisle.

Either walk through the village or take the river-side path signed on the left walking until you reach the cross path then go right, over the bridge, up to the road and straight across into the lane opposite. Turn right when you reach the drive to Claypits Farm bridleway, signposted to Coombe Keynes and Winfrith. After passing the farm keep going along the stony grass track, into the field and straight ahead beside the hedge until it veers to the right at which point maintain your direction across the field roughly making for the midpoint, where a track descends gently downhill. In summer expect to see bright blue chicory, field scabious, corn camomile and greater knapweed. Keep straight on past the farm buildings, up the field to the gate and join the path ahead into Coombe Wood.

Go over the cross track and straight ahead on the main path. The woods are a mix of coniferous and deciduous trees with lots of bluebells and primroses. When the path reaches the field walk straight ahead, through the gap and turn left around the field, up through the half gate following the track to the road. Turn right and then next left to Coombe Keynes.

This delightful little village with its now redundant church, dedicated to the Holy Rood, is a good example of a medieval nucleated village. Keynes is from the family name of the lords of the manor from the 12th to the 14th century. A walk up to the church is worthwhile to view the medieval font which, although plain, was drawn by a certain 21 year-old Thomas Hardy in 1861. (see booklet in church for his drawing).

Continue through the village until you reach the right-hand bend at which point branch left and join the signposted bridleway. Keep straight ahead on this easy to follow route eventually arriving at a wooden gate. The sandy but sometimes wet path beyond descends gently through a coniferous wood fringed with coppiced hazel eventually meeting a cross track. Turn left here, bridleway signposted to Wood Street. Follow this primrose-fringed gully up between the trees and onto the track at the top. Although overgrown in summer a bonus is the multitude of meadow brown butterflies. Further on the track widens before reaching the lane.

Turn right along this quiet lane which wends its way between old farm buildings and woods. At the junction with Bindon Lane walk straight ahead, around the bend before taking a footpath on the right signposted, 'East Stoke'. Bear half right across the field making for the east end of the woods ahead, keeping to the edge of the wood until it changes direction. Make for a clump of trees to your left (the distant church tower stands to the right of it). At the SW corner of the clump a gap in the trees reveals the ruins of the old church of St Mary, East Stoke.

The ruins of St. Mary's, East Stoke, slowly being consumed by the undergrowth.

The ruins of St. Mary's, showing stoup bowl on shaft in foreground.

The church's dedication was recorded in 1306 but by Hutchin's time the church was already in decay. He recorded "…a small portion of the old church remains in its churchyard as a memorial to it". There was formerly a nave, chancel, porch and tower but much of the stone was removed to build the new church in 1828. What remains now is a section of the south wall of the nave and the south porch, all being gradually consumed by the endless march of time and vegetation. Sections of ornate arches can be seen lying about, which formerly adorned windows and the entrance to the porch until they fell down between 1948-63. Of interest is the stoup set into the porch wall. It is mounted on a shaft and has a recess above. This was formerly a receptacle for holy water, placed near the church door for self-conse-cration and spiritual cleansing. It remains today as a sort of symbolic votive offering bowl, perhaps for the modern pilgrim to utilise. Look also for the scratch sundial and a block of fallen stone with a skull and cross-bones carved on it. This little known ruin, surrounded as it is by encroaching ivy and brambles, is a place of peace, reflection and solitude. The Roman temple at the start of this pilgrimage is linked to these ruins by Man's desire to express and practice his spiritual ideals. The buildings are separated in time by hundreds of years yet, today, you have bridged the eons of time with your very footsteps.

❖❖❖❖❖❖❖❖❖❖❖❖❖❖❖❖❖❖❖❖❖❖❖❖❖❖❖❖

Silent, forgotten stones,
Entwined by ivy and barbed bramble,
consuming the efforts and faith of those
Long since fallen on sleep.
Moss and lichen compete on decaying column
And fallen arch.
Am I at an ancient temple, in far off jungle,
Discovering a long-lost civilisation?
I sit midst sentinels of collapsing stone and
Frost-shattered mortar, being slowly
Engorged by nature and time.
Man's transient ways and whims here laid bare,
Testimony to changing and declining faith.
Time he marches on, relentless and merciless,
Yet you, stones, stand here to guard the
Doors of my enquiring conscience.
Man moves on, leaving you behind,
But your spirit remains, enduring,
Solid as the stones before me.
I feel it. And I humbled.
'Ruins in the Woods' by Peter Knight.

❖❖❖❖❖❖❖❖❖❖❖❖❖❖❖❖❖❖❖❖❖❖❖❖❖❖❖

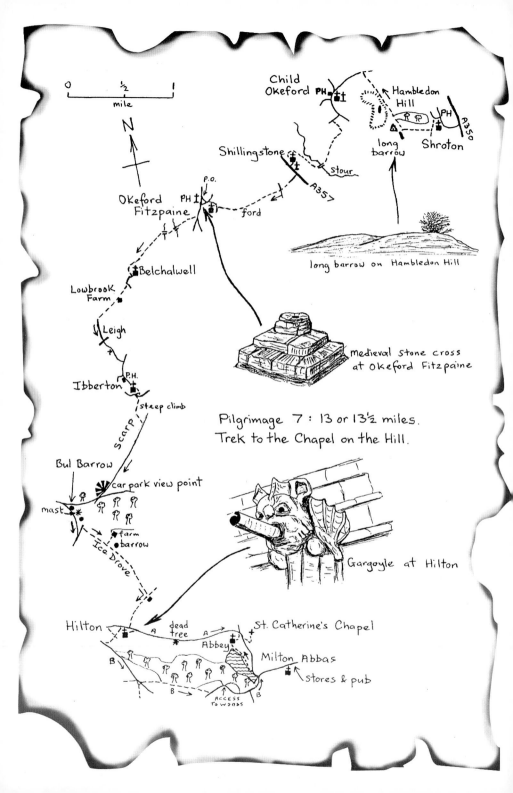

0 ½ 1
mile

N

Child
Okeford PH ⛪
Hambledon
Hill

Shroton PH ⛪ A350

long
barrow

Shillingstone ⛪
Stour

A357
ford

P.O.
Okeford PH †
Fitzpaine

long barrow on Hambledon Hill

Belchalwell

Lowbrook
Farm

Leigh

Ibberton P.H.

steep climb

Scarp

medieval stone cross
at Okeford Fitzpaine

Pilgrimage 7 : 13 or 13½ miles.
Trek to the Chapel on the Hill.

Bul Barrow

car park view point

mast

farm
barrow

Ice Drove

Gargoyle at Hilton

Hilton
dead
tree A
Abbey

St. Catherine's Chapel

Milton Abbas
stores & pub

B

B

ACCESS
TO WOODS

B

PILGRIMAGE SEVEN

TREK TO THE CHAPEL ON THE HILL

Park opposite the churchyard at Shroton, also known as Iwerne Courtney, north of Blandford.

A pilgrimage offering exhilarating views with high hills and plunging scarps. Prehistoric barrows, hill forts, interesting church architecture and old stone crosses are passed, culminating in the beauty of Milton Abbas. The walk has two steep climbs, one up Hambledon Hill, the other up the scarp to Bulbarrow. No shortage of refreshment stops on this walk. The Cricketers in Shroton itself is a good place for lunch, and there are pubs in Child Okeford, Shillingstone, Okeford Fitzpaine, Ibberton and the very atmospheric Hambro Arms in Milton Abbas.

OS Maps: Landranger 194, Explorer 117 and 118. Reference: 860/125.

Approximate distance: Approximate distance: 13 or 13½ miles. Ibberton Hill would be an appropriate point for a split walk.

We begin our journey at the church at Shroton. Note the dragon-winged gargoyles on the church as you cross to the south-west corner of the churchyard, to a small enclosed, open-air shrine. A fine Celtic-style cross, dated 1900, is the focus and the woods behind add to the peacefulness of the locality. Inside the church look for the three tiny Green Man images carved in wooden bosses in the eaves. We will encounter this ancient symbol of the earth later.

Walk back out of the main gate, turn left then left again. On the bend take the bridleway on the left which ascends behind the church. As one approaches woods take the bridleway on the right, up the slope of Hambledon Hill.

Approaching the ridge one can discern the earthworks of a Neolithic settlement, which developed into Iron Age fortifications. The sanctity of the hill in ancient times is borne out by the survival of two long barrows on the summit. They appear as long mounds, 6 – 7 feet high, either side of the Spur. The Eastern one (east of trig. Point) is aligned NW-SE, the Summer Solstice sunset and the Winter Solstice sunrise.

Hambledon Hill has folklore legends associated with it. The Druids were said to have planted a sacred yew grove, and the hill is said to protect the villages of Stourpaine and Durweston by supernatural forces. The hill would have been seen as the prone body of the Earth Goddess in ancient times with pilgrims making the ascent for sacred ceremonies.

Cross the spur and follow the north side of the earthworks with excellent vistas to the north. Look out for birds riding the thermals. The bridlepath descends steeply and we take the path left towards Child Okeford. The track turns into tarmac and we walk south to the centre of the village.

Hambledon Hill, seen from the churchyard at Shillingstone.

Opposite the pub is the village cross, a modern one that replaced a small megalith seen by Alfred Pope prior to 1906. The importance of the locality in former times is indicated by evidence that three ley lines intersect in the vicinity of the cross and the nearby church (see AS Fig. 128). A visit to the church reveals dragon stonework and a red dragon in a window, both common occurrences on leys, the 'dragon lines' of old. Note the Star of Solomon and other esoteric symbols near the altar, in elaborate marbling.

From the cross continue south through the village, taking the next right, the road to Sturninster Marshall and Shillingstone, then take the track left soon encountered. Follow it as it turns right and join the first footpath encountered, heading SW towards Shillingstone, whose church seen in the distance is our next destination. The path reaches a footbridge over the meandering River Stour, a tranquil spot to rest awhile. The other side of the river the path reaches the old railway cutting. Turn right and follow it west then take the next path left, forking left at the path intersection until Shillingstone church is reached.

From the churchyard the view north across the Stour Valley reveals Hambledon Hill rising majestically, with its earthworks visible on the skyline. Shillingstone church itself has a plain exterior, with modern tower and clock. To the SE of the chancel can be found the base of a 15th century stone cross (see AS plate 140). The main interest inside the church is the inscribed stone slab, fixed to the wall near the bell ropes (see AS plate 141 & SD page 160). The solar and lunar symbols either side of a Celtic-style head make it an esoteric work, the balance of left and right, lunar and solar, yin and yang.

Leave the churchyard at the main east entrance and turn right down to the main road where the magnificent 'high' stone cross is located.

The shaft and head date from 1903 but the base and steps are the original 15th century structure. Sitting on the steps, it is worth a pause to wonder at how many generations of people, many no doubt pilgrims, have sat here before you over something like 500 years.

Walk south through the village, passing the stores, turning right along the gravel path opposite Portman Hall. Continue along a grass path and through two small gates, turning right onto a tarmac drive. Turn left, following the drive and then footpaths west. Cross Puxey Lane to the signposted footpath opposite and over the field, bearing slightly right down the slope. The well-defined footpath continues west via gates and stiles to a ford. Bear right and follow the wide track (Pound Lane) west. On reaching Okeford Fitzpaine church, turn right and then left to enter the churchyard.

The cross at Shillingstone.

The exterior and inside of the church is plain and mainly restored, a date of 1866 given on the porch. If it is sunny then you could check the accuracy of the sundial. The chief interest here is that the church stands on one of the same leys as that of Child Okeford we passed through earlier. The ley, plotted by earth mysteries pioneer John Michell some years ago, runs from Two Gates Stones (Pilgrimage 1) right up to the sacred hill of Old Sarum, north of Salisbury (see AS fig. 128). Inside, another small Green Man adorns a roof bass.

Proceed to the village centre where, opposite the stores, stands the remains of the medieval stone cross.

Two steps and a socket stone survive, the shaft long gone. The Abbots of Glastonbury provided for services at the cross up to the time of Henry VIII. A plaque next to the cross provides historical information.

Take the road south out of the village. Just past the new estate of Fippenny Hollow, cross the stile on the opposite side of the road next to the last building. The initial stretch of the path can be somewhat overgrown in summer, but things soon improve. The path crosses fields and two small streams on its way to

99

The picturesque approach and exterior of Belchalwell church. Note the gargoyles up the tower.

Belchalwell church, which can be seen in the distance on a small rise. The path approaches the church from the north after skirting the churchyard.

This isolated spot is peaceful and the exterior of St Aldhelm's, dating from the 12th century, blends in with the serenity of the locality. Nice horned gargoyles adorn the architecture and note also two ancient heads either side of the door in the porch. The internal plastered and restored décor seem out of place here, but nevertheless peace and shelter are afforded to the pilgrim. The church in fact stands on the same ley line as was mentioned at Okeford Fitzpaine and Child Okeford (see AS fig. 128 for details). Of interest is the fine gargoyle halfway up the tower on the NE side. It gazes towards Hambledon on the skyline but it also stares along the ley already discussed. Peter Knight recently found a similarly positioned gargoyle halfway up the tower of Christchurch Priory, looking along the ley to St Catherine's Hill (see AS figs. 21 and 22). From Belchalwell churchyard we can also look north to Banbury Hill Fort with Piddles Wood beyond. To the east we can view the steep chalk scarp of Bell Hill. The name is possibly derived from the ancient sun god Belenus. The hill is capped with ancient barrows and settlements, and it is this scarp that we are to ascend and follow to Bulbarrow.

Walk along the church approach lane to the road, turn left and then next right, the track to Lowbrook Farm. Go through the farm, passing through three metal gates. Cross the next field to a gate, then across another meadow, through the gate and along the path keeping close to the hedge on your left. Turn left onto tarmac road keeping straight ahead at the crossroads towards Ibberton. Turn right at the junction then left at the centre of the village, signposted 'Halter Path to Church'.

The stone head with horns at Ibberton church. It is the only surviving gargoyle.

Worth a visit, the Crown Inn, built between the 15th and 16th century, originally had just one small bar with a cosy snug, the rear bar being added fairly recently. The bar still has its original flagstone floor and large inglenook fireplace. Hanging from the mantle are some unusual Burmese prayer gongs.

Continue up the steep climb, passing under shady trees and climbing old stone steps to the church.

This mainly restored church affords fine views from its high position. Inside look for the griffin in one of the SW facing windows and the sun symbol in the window near the font. Powerful earth energies have been dowsed in the church by Jenny and Jack Cummings. Outside, look for the two stone carvings either side of the NW facing window next to the tower. One appears to have horns and is clearly non-human (illustrated here).

Resume the path upward and round the back of the church. Cross the road and go through the gate opposite. Follow the well-defined bridleway south as it gradually ascends the steep scarp, keeping close to the hedge. Turn half-left just past a line of trees and head up the slope to a clump of large trees. Go through the gate behind the trees, turning right onto the road and follow it south, bearing right at the staggered junction to Bulbarrow (grid ref. 775/057).

This famous barrow is barely discernible now, a low mound near the junction NW of the intrusive mast. It is covered with impenetrable gorse now yet the barrow was placed with great care, enabling distant views of other sacred places. At 902 feet, this is in fact the second highest place in all of Dorset. To the north Glastonbury Tor rises out of the Somerset Levels, some 27 miles away. A gap in the hedgerow enables a view west, with Rawlsbury Camp half a mile along the scarp. Beyond that the woods of Melcombe Park stand out, with

Fine gargoyles on the north side of Hilton church.

Church Hill and Nettlecombe Tout, another hill fort, beyond. The intricacy by which our distant ancestors laid out their sacred sites on the landscape can here be wonderfully demonstrated. The settlements and earthworks at Grimstone Down, Nettlecombe Tout, Rawlsbury Camp and Hambledon Hill all lie in a straight line. Incredibly, this ley aligns with the summer solstice sunrise! (See SD fig. 2).

Walk south along the road, past the mast and turn sharp left at the junction, temporarily heading north. A gate is soon encountered on the right, signposted to Hilton and Milton Abbey. Take this bridle track. A scarp plunges below us for nearly a mile. Just beyond the farm track a round barrow lies in the field to the north. The solitude of this little-travelled track is refreshing and the views uplifting west and south. At Hilton Hill Buildings turn right, descending the hill to Hilton. Upon reaching the road visit the church of All Saints opposite.

The survival of Saxon and Norman architecture makes this church interesting. The fine porch roof is noteworthy and inside note the medieval painted panels of the Apostles, and glimpses of old stonework. On the outside note the winged gargoyles on the tower and on the north side of the chancel. On the other side note a sundial and alms tables on the south wall.

From here the pilgrim has two options. Route A is easier as the road eastwards into Milton Abbey is taken. Note the large dead tree at grid reference: 791/026, on the south side of the road. How many faces can you see in the dead sentinel? Route B offers a half mile longer walk, yet is quieter with a lakeside walk at the end. We go west along the road from the church, turning next left along the bridleway.

Continue straight ahead ignoring side paths and tracks, uphill until the woods are reached following the path through, then across the field and out to the road.

Turn left heading south up Coombe Hill and just past the bend take the track on the left. This peaceful bridleway skirts the woods of Monmouth Hill for ¾ mile until a tarred lane is encountered. Turn left following it into Milton Abbey. The walk passes woods, and a long, ancient wall of flints before reaching the main road.

Keep straight ahead skirting the south end of the lake walking past the bottom of the village. At the junction one can look up and see the famous white painted thatched cottages that line both sides of the street. But we take the road left, signposted Abbey. On the bend take the path left marked Abbey Church only. This beautiful path takes us alongside the lake, which was designed by Capability Brown in the 18th century, and on to the abbey.

The coolness and peace of Milton Abbey may be welcome indeed to the possibly now-wearying pilgrim. Founded by Athelstan of Wessex circa 933-938 the present abbey is largely 15th century, following a fire, which damaged much of the Norman building which preceded it. Booklets obtainable in the abbey tell of its history and that of the village. Of relevance to us is certainly the stone bust of St James of Compostella, in the Lady Chapel. He is the patron saint of pilgrims, his image linking us with those who have come this way before over hundreds of years.

The lake at Milton Abbas.

Two relics of Milton Abbey.
A: Winged creature on porch.
B: Bust of pilgrims' patron saint
in Lady Chapel.

Back outside, note the winged creatures returning your gaze at the corner of the porch. Dragon-like and other winged gargoyles commonly occur on church architecture when the churches are on ley lines, the dragon lines of old (see SD page 252 onwards for discussion and examples). Milton Abbey stands on two leys, one of which links the abbey with Cattistock, on Pilgrimage 2 (see AS figs. 36 & 118 for details).

Walk back around the south side of the abbey.

At the south-east corner of the lawns a small bush shades the socket stone of a 15th century market cross. In its heyday it had 30 ascending steps, a grandiose structure indeed. A painting in the abbey shows the cross in its original position, where market traders vended their wares midst the hustle and bustle on market days.

The medieval stone cross east of the abbey at Milton Abbas, shaded under a small tree.

Walk round the east end of the lawns, noting the grass steps, one of only two in the country. They head directly up to the Chapel of St Catherine, our pilgrimage destination, although they are not now open to the public. On reaching the school car park turn right back to the road. Turning left walk north until a track on the right is reached, then follow it up through the woods to St Catherine's Chapel (follow the signs on trees taking a sharp left where tracks meet).

St Catherine is the patron saint of unmarried girls, spinsters and hilltops. The wheel, which she is associated with, can be related to the wheel of the turning year, with its eight divisions, seen in stone at Cerne Abbas well (Pilgrimage 4). She almost certainly replaced

a former earth Goddess, hence her link with hills, combining with the solar disc at the old fire festivals. The site is in legend that where Athelstan had his divine interventions on the eve of battle with the Danes. In the 12th century the Norman's rebuilt the chapel which was obviously a shrine for pilgrims for the 12th century inscription grants 120 days indulgence, a common practice at medieval shrines.

St. Catherine's Chapel, nestling in the woods above Milton Abbey.

below: Milton Abbey, seen from St Catherine's Chapel.

Some believe that the chapel was also used by women, who were not allowed into the monastic abbey below, or else the foundation was some monastic cell which had fallen into ruin by Athelstan's time. Whatever the true origins of the chapel, the locality is clearly mysterious and sacred. The abbey can be viewed below and one feels a sanctity that transgresses all faiths, all creeds and all of time. Abbeys and religions come and go, but the land remains, eternal and forever giving. In this wood, at this chapel, the old meets the new, and both seem to live in quiet acceptance.

❖❖❖❖❖❖❖❖❖❖❖❖❖❖❖❖❖❖❖❖❖❖❖❖❖❖

"A husband, St Catherine,
A handsome one, St Catherine,
A rich one, St Catherine
A nice one, St Catherine,
And soon, St Catherine!"
(Old Dorset Charm)

❖❖❖❖❖❖❖❖❖❖❖❖❖❖❖❖❖❖❖❖❖❖❖❖❖❖

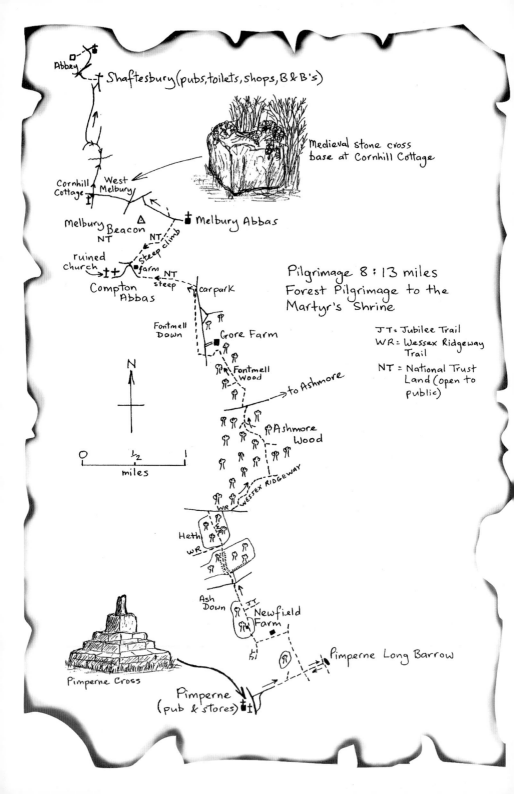

Abbey

Shaftesbury (pubs, toilets, shops, B & B's)

Medieval stone cross
base at Cornhill Cottage

Cornhill
Cottage

West
Melbury

Melbury Abbas

Melbury Beacon
NT

NT. steep climb

ruined
church

farm

NT
steep

Compton
Abbas

carpark

Fontmell
Down

Gore Farm

Pilgrimage 8 : 13 miles
Forest Pilgrimage to the
Martyr's Shrine

JT = Jubilee Trail
WR = Wessex Ridgeway
Trail
NT = National Trust
Land (open to
public)

Fontmell
Wood

→ to Ashmore

Ashmore
Wood

N

WESSEX RIDGEWAY

0   ½   1
        miles

WR

Heth

WR

Ash
Down

JT

Newfield
Farm

Pimperne Long Barrow

Pimperne Cross

Pimperne
(pub & stores)

PILGRIMAGE EIGHT

FOREST PILGRIMAGE TO THE MARTYR'S SHRINE

Park at Pimperne church, under the grand old sycamore close to the ancient cross.

OS Maps: Landranger 195 and Explorer 118.
Reference: 905/094.

An enjoyable pilgrimage for the most part on well-established bridleways. Whilst quite hilly in places the going is generally good underfoot and not over strenuous. Some sections however are heavily rutted and can be very muddy in the winter. The best time is the end of April when the bluebell woods are at their most beautiful. Refreshment is only available at the start at the Anvil Inn and various pubs at the finish. There are tea rooms at the top of Gold Hill.

Approximate distance:
13 miles. Although past the half way point, the car park east of Compton Abbas can be used for a split walk.

The Celts were the first to settle here beside the river with 'five trees', thus named PIM-PREN. The Manor was later owned by Henry VIII and given to his fifth wife Catherine Howard. After she was beheaded ownership transferred to Catherine Parr.

The ancient stone cross at Pimperne nestles under the shade of a grand old sycamore.

107

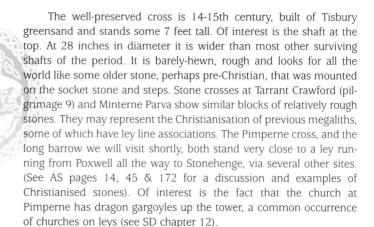

The well-preserved cross is 14-15th century, built of Tisbury greensand and stands some 7 feet tall. Of interest is the shaft at the top. At 28 inches in diameter it is wider than most other surviving shafts of the period. It is barely-hewn, rough and looks for all the world like some older stone, perhaps pre-Christian, that was mounted on the socket stone and steps. Stone crosses at Tarrant Crawford (pilgrimage 9) and Minterne Parva show similar blocks of relatively rough stones. They may represent the Christianisation of previous megaliths, some of which have ley line associations. The Pimperne cross, and the long barrow we will visit shortly, both stand very close to a ley running from Poxwell all the way to Stonehenge, via several other sites. (See AS pages 14, 45 & 172 for a discussion and examples of Christianised stones). Of interest is the fact that the church at Pimperne has dragon gargoyles up the tower, a common occurrence of churches on leys (see SD chapter 12).

Walk north away from the village and soon turn right into Arlecks Lane. Go straight on at the top, carry on through the gates and up the tarred drive ahead walking all the way along the track to the corner. Divert the short distance ahead to reach Pimperne long barrow.

Looking SE along the axis of the Pimperne Long Barrow. This is aligned to the mid winter sunrise, which rises over the hill on the skyline, where more barrows stand.

This Neolithic mound is around 4500-5500 years old and is one of the biggest in Dorset. It is 350 feet long, having a breadth of 90 feet and still about 9 feet high. It is parallel-sided with prominent side ditches. A berm, or platform, on the sides of the mound may have assisted astronomical observations and the locality of the barrow was

chosen with great care, with distant views. For it is now accepted that these ancient mounds were very much used by the living and not just the dead. The barrow is very close to a ley running almost exactly east-west, equinox-aligned, linking the Verwood megalith, Knowlton and Hod Hill. The barrow is self-aligned NW-SE, the winter solstice sunrise and summer solstice sunset. Looking SE along the axis of the mound one can see a hill on the skyline, which is capped by settlement earthworks and another long barrow (not visible). It is over this hill that the midwinter sun rises when viewed from this barrow. The axis of the barrow was also aligned to the rising of Sirius, the brightest star, so important in Neolithic times. This bright star is linked with the Egyptian god Isis.

The beauty and solitude of the pilgrim's path through the forest.

Return to the corner, turn right and continue round the field and along the track, down through the gate to the end of the field turning left onto the gravel track. Turn right at Handcock's Bottom onto the signposted bridleway. Fork right further on by the dwelling. Carry on a long this peaceful grass and mud track which rises steadily to the road. Cross over to the bridleway opposite.

We continue north through lovely woods in which you can expect to see a lovely springtime display of bluebells, primroses, white wood anemones and large fronds of green spurge. The path then follows the edge of the field beside a delightful bluebell wood home also to early purple spotted orchids. Further on follow the bridleway into the wood on the right which rises to the road. Turn right and, keeping to the right-hand side,

109

walk downhill until you reach the signed path on the left. Make your way up and round the field staying close to the edge of the wood until a signed path takes you into the Hanging Coppice. After descending gradually to the Stubhampton Bottom turn left onto the bridle track which further on merges with a well-surfaced forest track. Maintain direction keeping to the main track, rising steadily to the road at Washers Pit.

Turn left and almost immediately take the signed bridle-way on the right. Fenced on both sides the ridged grass track rises steadily into Fontmell Wood. Ignore the bridleway on the left but continue following the narrow track ahead, which rises through tranquil areas of bluebells and white garlic ransoms competing for every inch of available space. Walk round to the grass track, turn right and leave by the gate into the road.

Carefully cross to the gate opposite and go down the field keeping close to the fence, through the gate at the bottom and turn right. The ground slips away steeply to the west and Fontmell Down, an area of outstanding natural beauty rises up the other side of the valley. Walk north parallel with the road, cross the stile and follow the clearly defined track and path leading to the small car park. Take the wide track on the left which descends steeply in places, offering fine views, down to East Compton.

The approach to East Compton. The remains of the old church, our next destination, are to the right.

The ancient stone cross and remaining tower of the former church at East Compton.

This cluster of cottages and a farm nestles below steep scarps, which protect it on three sides. The tower is all that remains of the old St Mary's church replaced now by the newer one at Compton Abbas, ½ mile west. The old churchyard is somewhat neglected and atmospheric. South of the tower stands the remnants of a 15th century stone cross. The steps and socket stone are capped by 18inches of shaft, and the structure offers an ancient resting place for the modern pilgrim.

Walk north through the village and join the bridleway on the right signposted, Melbury Abbas ¾. Gentle at first but after passing through the gate and crossing the field to the gate opposite the track rises fairly steeply up Melbury Hill, home to numerous cowslips. Before reaching the top peel off to the left and head for the small wooden gate. Looking left, Melbury Beacon rises, with ancient earthworks and cross dykes. Follow the beaten path beyond down the hillside to the small gate in the hedge at the bottom. Keep straight ahead across the field to the gate on the far side, making for the church of St Thomas.

Melbury Abbas has a long history of settlement. Roman remains have been found locally but it was the Anglo-Saxons who first settled here. The Doomsday Book records a thriving population of over 200 and 4 mills. As the name suggests, the village was owned by

The church at Melbury Abbas.

Shaftesbury Abbey until its dissolution in 1539. The church was rebuilt by the Victorians, yet has some interesting stone work suggesting more ancient symbologies. A winged lion, griffin-like gargoyles and other beasts decorate the church's exterior. A huge yew at least 300 years old stands on the east side of the central path, giving welcome shade to the pilgrim. Set into the tarmac path just west of the lych-gate and only discovered in 1999 is a 3½ foot wide stone. It appears to be of local greensand and is roughly heart-shaped. Ancient stones have been found elsewhere in Dorset in the vicinity of churches, suggesting the Christianisation of earlier sacred places. Other examples of such stones can be seen at the churches of Whitcombe (pilgrimage 5), Toller Porcorum (pilgrimage 1) and Knowlton (pilgrimage 9).

Turn back along Quarry (School) Lane out of the village, up to the junction, turn left and then next right. Carefully cross the busy A350 into the lane opposite, walking as far as the crossroads at West Melbury.

The large stone (in the foreground) at Melbury Abbas (photo: Andrew Lane, used with permission).

below: The ancient stone cross base at Cornhill Cottage.

Gold Hill, Shaftesbury.

The socket stone of a medieval stone stands behind the yew hedge in the front garden of Cornhill Cottage but is not visible from the road. (Permission should be sought to view). At one time the cross stood at the nearby crossroads, on the north-south pilgrims way from south Dorset to the monastery at Shaftesbury. The locality may have an even more ancient heritage, for it has been shown previously how the crossroads lies on a ley line running up from Bind Barrow in south Dorset right up to Stonehenge itself, via several other sites (see AS figs. 120 & 132).

From the crossroads take the lane north down to the stream and then steeply up French Mill Lane, ignoring the turning on the right. Take the next right following it almost up to the junction. On the left behind the letterbox is a very attractive narrow path, which drops gently down to a track. Keep straight ahead up into Kingsman Lane then turn right into the road and take the next left ascending the famous Gold Hill. The cobbled

street has cottages on one side and the buttressed precinct wall of the abbey on the other. At the top of the hill Shaftesbury Abbey, our final destination, is signposted off to the left.

The site of the abbey is certainly a fitting end to any pilgrimage as indeed it has been for hundreds of years. The Benedictine abbey was founded in AD 888 by King Alfred the Great who installed his daughter Aethelgifu, as the first Abbess. The abbey owed a lot of its fortune to the many pilgrims visiting the shrine of St Edward, King and Martyr who was murdered at Corfe Castle by his step-mother and brought to rest at the abbey. The Danish King Canute and Catherine of Aragon both stayed here when the abbey was at its height. At the Dissolution, in 1539, the abbey was abandoned and the stone soon fell prey to the new owners, who used much of it in buildings around the town.

Perhaps at the end of this pilgrimage, you will find your own place in the abbey to sit and ponder and reflect on your journey. Thousands have visited this place before you, yet the experience of every pilgrim is unique. For this is the nature of pilgrimage, as it reflects not only the uniqueness of every second in time, but also the uniqueness of every person on this planet.

A new museum was officially opened on the 2 May 1999 housing a fascinating collection of carved stonework including gargoyles, horned creatures and medieval floor tiles with symbolic designs. A small admission charge allows you to wander freely around the excavated remains of this important monument following numbered pegs in the grounds. Norman stonework, stone coffins, altars and Edward's shrine are all impressive. Please note that opening times are usually from April to October only. (Tel 01747 852910 for details).

The remains of Shaftesbury Abbey, the pilgrimage destination.

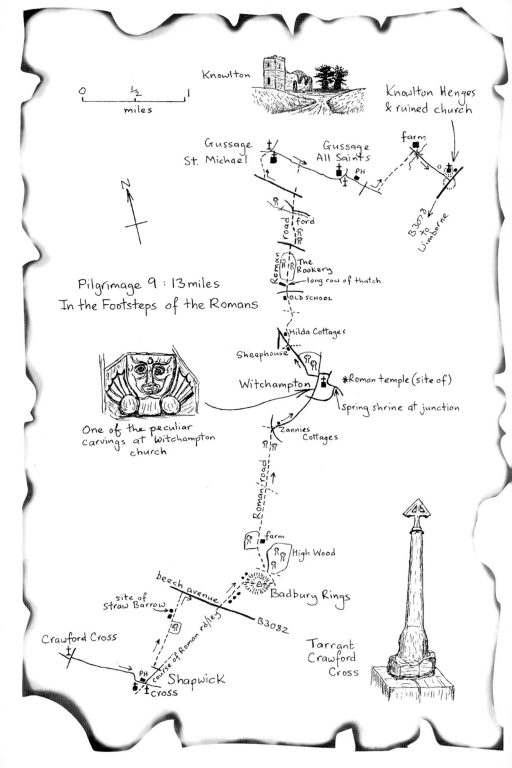

Knowlton

Knowlton Henges
& ruined church

0   ½   1
miles

Gussage
St. Michael

Gussage
All Saints

PH

farm

B3078 to Wimborne

Roman road

ford

The Rookery
—long row of thatch.

OLD SCHOOL

Pilgrimage 9 : 13 miles
In the Footsteps of the Romans

N

Hilda Cottages

Sheephouse

Witchampton

*Roman temple (site of)

spring shrine at junction

One of the peculiar
carvings at Witchampton
church

Zannies Cottages

Roman road

farm

High Wood

beech avenue

site of
Straw Barrow

Badbury Rings

B3082

course of Roman rd/ley

Crawford Cross

PH

Shapwick

Cross

Tarrant
Crawford
Cross

IN THE FOOTSTEPS OF THE ROMANS

Park by the ancient cross, which is on an old pilgrimage track between the former abbey at Tarrant Crawford and Wimborne Minster.

This pilgrimage offers perhaps the easiest walking of the ten, with few steep gradients and long stretches of straight track as it follows Roman roads along three stretches. The walk combines an interesting blend of old crosses, churches, Roman fords and a hill fort, culminating at Knowlton, one of the major sacred complexes of prehistoric Dorset. Refreshments are available at The Anchor Inn, Shapwick about a mile from the start and also The Drovers Inn at Gussage All Saints about a mile and a half from the finish.

OS Maps: Landranger 195 and Explorer 118.
Reference: 924/028.

Approximate distance:
13 miles. Witchampton is ideal for a split walk.

above: The cross at Shapwick. The steps and base stone are 15th century.

The Crawford Cross is one of the best contenders for an ancient megalith that was Christianised at a later date. The 15th century eroded plinth supports a mainly modern shaft and head, but the lowest 1 foot 10 inches of shaft are older, bulbous and very rough, resembling a more ancient stone (see AS plate 11). The cross shaft at Minterne Parva is likewise shaped, much wider than the typical shaft of the period. The cross at Child Okeford replaced a stone seen by Alfred Pope prior to 1906 (see pilgrimage 7). A 19th century sketch by John Baverstock Knight of the Crawford Cross shows the stump of stone on a low mound, with Spetisbury Rings in the background (see Harte, 1986, Page 4).

From the cross take the road to Shapwick taking care along the narrow stretch for the first quarter of a mile. Hedgerows thick with cow parsley keep the walker company, along with tall

left: Shapwick Church.

feathery grasses. At the village of Shapwick stop at the Anchor Inn, and view the cross opposite.

The old 15th century base and steps are surmounted now by a modern plinth and shaft. Running approximately north-south past the cross is the route of the Roman road, connecting Dorchester with Badbury Rings. To the south of the church the road crossed the Stour via a ford. It has been demonstrated previously (AS Fig. 49) how the Roman road passes prehistoric sites, the line ultimately being project-ed past Dorchester to the Hellstone, a Neolithic long barrow (Pilgrimage 3). This invites the suggestion that the Romans simply up-graded a route, which had originated as a ley alignment. So perhaps the Shapwick Cross originally replaced either a Roman stone or pre-historic megalith. The nearby church of St. Bartholomew is worth a visit to view its Norman arches, elaborate font cover and some sur-viving Saxon stonework in the exterior walls west of the north porch.

Back at the crossroads walk north east along High Street. At the crossroads, where Ram Lane and Park Lane meet, take a left and walk a short distance up the roughly tarred road. Turn right at Elm Tree cottage onto the well-defined track that is Swan Way. This soon opens out into open country, gradually ascend-ing to Swan Way Copse.

Just past the cottage on the left is a low mound. This is the sad vestige of Straw Barrow, a Bronze Age round barrow excavated in 1838, which contained many huge blocks of sandstone. In the 1960's some blocks were still lying around, but now have all been removed (see AS plate 22 for drawing of excavation). A ley line running from Mupe Bay up to Stonehenge passes just yards east of the barrow, and dowsing has detected energy lines at the site.

Continue along the track until the main road is reached then turn right and make your way along the avenue of beeches.

Planted in 1835, originally there were 365 trees, one for every day of the year, but storms have reduced their numbers. Several barrows used to line the road denoting a ley (AS fig. 39).

Turn left into the entrance to Badbury Rings and make your way over stiles to the summit climbing over earthen banks built to repel the Romans.

The Roman road we stood on at Shapwick crosses the field on our right and three barrows can be seen in a line close to it. They align parallel with the Roman route and may have stood originally by a pre-Roman track (AS fig. 49). Vespasian and his army duly conquered the hill fort in AD 43-44 for it lies only three miles from the legion's base

camp at Lake Farm. The area is peppered with round barrows and hills such as this would most likely have been utilised for more spiritual purposes prior to being fortified. Some claim Badbury Rings to be the site of Mons Baden, where Arthur defeated the invading Anglo-Saxons. The hill is a place of mystery and in fact apparitions and folklore are associated with the area (see SD pages 126 & 196).

Looking east along the avenue of Beeches.

below: The spring shrine at Witchampton, opposite a Roman temple and on a ley.

Leave the hill fort via the eastern path and descend the earthworks until a north-south bridleway is reached. Follow this left (north), over a stile walking with High Wood to your right. At King Down we join the course of a Roman road again and remain in the footsteps of the Romans for over a mile. Just past Little Coppice the bridleway leaves the ancient road coming out at a small crossroads. Go straight ahead past Zannies Cottages on the left and on to the village of Witchampton.

At the next crossroads turn right descending towards the River Allen. The road bears left and at the next junction an ancient spring shrine will be found.

119

Victorian and 18th century stonework surrounds a much older altar-like stone, with a tiny hole where once the waters flowed. No one can date the structure, but the fact that a Roman temple once stood in an adjacent field, and that the shrine and nearby church are both on a ley alignment, points to a very ancient sacred locality. In ancient times waters issuing from the ground were revered as the blessings and gift of the Earth's Goddess, from whose womb the waters flowed. It has been shown that some of Dorset's curative wells and springs are located on ley lines, such as Upwey, Cranborne and Cerne Abbas, to name but three. (For a discussion on the wells/ley link see SD pages 104-114).

From the crossroads walk up the hill and around the bend to the church.

Note how it stands prominently on a mound, echoing other churches that were built on more ancient sites such as Knowlton, Church Knowle and Toller Porcorum. Winged dragon gargoyles up the tower once again denote a church on a ley alignment. The ley runs up from Tyneham, via Wareham, Bradford Barrow, Witchampton and three barrows near the Dorset Cursus, all the way to Stonehenge. Inside the church are two of the most unusual medieval carvings in Dorset. Upon entering the church look up on either side of you where you will see two carved heads. Pre-Christian symbolism is evident in both, such as spheres with dragon wings, Egyptian-like beards, phallic noses and third-eye symbols on the forehead (see drawing on map of this pilgrimage and also SD plate 31). Coming out of the church note the medieval male exhibitionist carving on the north-east corner of the tower, a type rare in the county.

The longest row of thatch in England, next to the route of the Roman road.

The tranquility of the woodland clearing in The Rookery.

Leave the churchyard via the top gate and continue along the road. Take the next left climbing the hill out of the village. At the junction turn left and then immediately right walking along the road that skirts Downley Coppice. At Sheephouse, ignore a footpath on the right and likewise pass by another on the left before taking the more well defined bridleway of

The Roman ford, NW of Moor Crichel.

Rowberry Lane on the right which winds its way north. After passing the Old School, we rejoin the Roman road again at the point we tread on tarmac road. Follow the track beside Drum Cottage with the Roman road underfoot. A magnificent and extremely long row of thatched cottages is soon encountered as we continue ahead skirting an open field, with the hedgerows on our right. Ignore the overgrown track and gate on the right, and enter The Rookery woods. One soon reaches a peaceful clearing, the air filled with butterflies and birdsong.

We continue in the footsteps of the Romans through woods and then across open ground until a road is encountered. The bridleway crosses the field opposite but sometimes during summer crops can restrict the path. For a pleasant alternative turn right along the road to The Lodge then join the gravel track north into the woods. After a bend to the right the track comes out into open ground where there are fine views to the east down into the valley north of Crichel Lake. The track soon approaches the woods again as it rejoins the Roman

road. We descend to the ford built by the Romans to cross the stream. One can pause here and imagine the legions plodding their way across on their way north to further conquests.

Leaving the ford walk briefly along the road and take the bridleway on the right signposted, Ringwood-Salisbury Rd 1/2 m. Follow this very scenic but sometimes overgrown track uphill, and over open ground to the road. Leave the Roman road and turn left. Look out for the yellow waymark on the right, cross the stile and take the path left downhill, via a small copse to Gussage St Michael. At the road turn right and walk to the crossroads and church of St Michael.

The arch dragon-slayer of Christian mythology, hundreds of churches across Europe were dedicated to this saint, in an attempt to stamp out the old pagan practices, which were very much associated with dragons. Serpents and dragons also symbolised earth energies as well as ley lines and the church was eager to eradicate knowledge of both. Inside the church there are stained-glass windows showing a winged bull and lion, old images which were adopted for St Luke and St Mark. To the left of the altar is an ante-room where St Michael can be seen slaying the British red dragon. (For a full discussion of dragon symbolism in Dorset architecture see SD chapters 1,2 & 12). Back at the crossroads, next to the letterbox, is the stump of a 14th/15th century stone cross. The cross in fact marks the intersection of two ley lines, surely indicating that the cross and nearby church replaced a pre-Christian sacred place, such as a stone perhaps. (See AS figs. 24 & 25).

Take the road east out of the village towards Gussage All Saints. After a little under half a mile a bridleway crosses the road. This is our last encounter with the Roman road we travelled along earlier. Called Ackling Dyke, it crosses the Dorset Cursus to the north before marching on to Salisbury.

At Gussage All Saints green the modern cross superseded a medieval one already lost prior to 1906. In the adjacent churchyard, near the church door, note the gravestone in the style of a Celtic cross, with delicate knotwork and interlacing. The church was largely rebuilt in 1864, but the tower is 15th century. There is a fine clock on the tower, yet no gargoyles. The interior of the church is quite plain, yet the fine stained-glass window behind the altar is worthy of closer inspection. The heads of an eagle, a lion and a bull, representing three of the Apostles, can be found, images adopted and adapted from pre-Christian times. The early Church used the 'pulling power' of pagan symbolism in an effort to fill its churches.

From the church continue east through the village past, or into, the Drovers Inn, a very good refreshment stop. At Amen Corner crossroads go straight across descending gradually into the river valley of the Allen. Turn left into Brockington Lane, marked as a public footpath. This grassy track yields occasional glimpses of Knowlton Church ruins, our pilgrimage destination. Just past some trees the path emerges into Lumber Lane. Turn right and follow the road over the River Allen and on to Knowlton.

The fine window, with animal symbology, at Gussage All Saints.

Knowlton is one of those places that stirs emotions, a capsule of eternity where one is readily transported back to times long past. Many find the atmosphere eerie, and indeed the rampant, strong earth energies of the place can have a variety of effects on different people. The centre henge was Christianised with a Norman church, now ruined, whilst other earthen henges nearby are now largely levelled (see AS pages 48-53 for site plans, photos and astronomical alignments). The mounds, with internal ditches, were built some 4000-4500 years ago, during the Neolithic. However the area contin-

The ruins of Knowlton church within the Neolithic henge. Two sacred yew trees stand to the left, whilst the Great Barrow, covered in trees, marks out equinox sunrises to the right.

ued to be used for ritual well into the Bronze Age, as judged by the numerous round barrows in the surrounding landscape. A huge Neolithic mound, covered in trees, can be seen in the field to the east. The equinox sun rises out of this mound and this can clearly be viewed as symbolic of the Sky God being born out of the tummy of the Earth Goddess (for a view of this spectacular event see SD plate 63).

Jacquetta Hawkes, archaeologist and widow of J B Priestley, once wrote of Knowlton:

"There is something peculiar in the air, an influence.....
perhaps one of those places where men have felt intensely......
and never quite rid themselves of the effects."

The earth energies, readily experienced by dowsers and the unaware alike, contribute much to the atmosphere Hawkes alludes to. Energy lines spiral in and out of the central henge, and most appear to make contact with the ruined church at some point. The buttresses, particularly, seem to attract a charge. The energies can be felt if these buttresses are held at certain places, with open palms, and open minds! (For details of energies, see AS page 50-51 and figs. 26 & 28). One strong band passes between the two yews, which are said to be over 2500 years old!

One result to come out of the dowsing by experienced dowsing groups is the strong probability that megaliths once stood in the henge. An outer and inner circle of stones seems likely, with a possible avenue heading off NE from the centre. This is echoed on a much vaster scale at Avebury. Some evidence discovered recently by Peter Knight may prove that stones once stood here. At the base of the tower, at the north corner, a long uncut stone lies horizontally at ground level. It is thicker one end, tapering to almost a point at the other. This could be one of the lost megaliths, symbolically underpinning the Christian church. The stone is of the same material as those at the Rempstone Stone Circle and the Agglestone (both on Pilgrimage 10).

Knowlton is a place hard to go away from, and a place that invites us back again and again. The locality is alive with earth energies, which ancient Man saw as living proof of an Earth Mother Goddess. Try if you can to return for a sunrise or else sit under the stars and moon. For Knowlton, like the land itself, displays many moods. Perhaps that is why us mortals can relate to the place. But perhaps more than that, it reminds us of the timelessness of the land and its inherent spirit. For we are all, ultimately, linked to both.

The large stone at the base of the tower at Knowlton. Is this one of the lost megaliths?

❖❖❖❖❖❖❖❖❖❖❖❖❖❖❖❖❖❖❖❖❖❖❖❖❖❖

Knowlton, Knowlton, cradle of knowing,
Mother Earth is putting on a showing.
Dowsing rods which swing and twitch,
As we tread the sacred mound and ditch.
Tell me, does your hair stand on end,
Does your trusty hazel twig bend?
Dancing cosmic joy, life of the land,
The crystal pendulum that spins from my hand.
Bare earth here, tinglings there,
Signs of the Dragon everywhere.
Sense the current, by night and day,
Through seasons never-ending, or so I pray,
Knowlton, Knowlton, how can I leave,
When the Web of Life you seem to weave.
(Extract from 'Knowlton Earth Rising', by Peter Knight)

❖❖❖❖❖❖❖❖❖❖❖❖❖❖❖❖❖❖❖❖❖❖❖❖❖

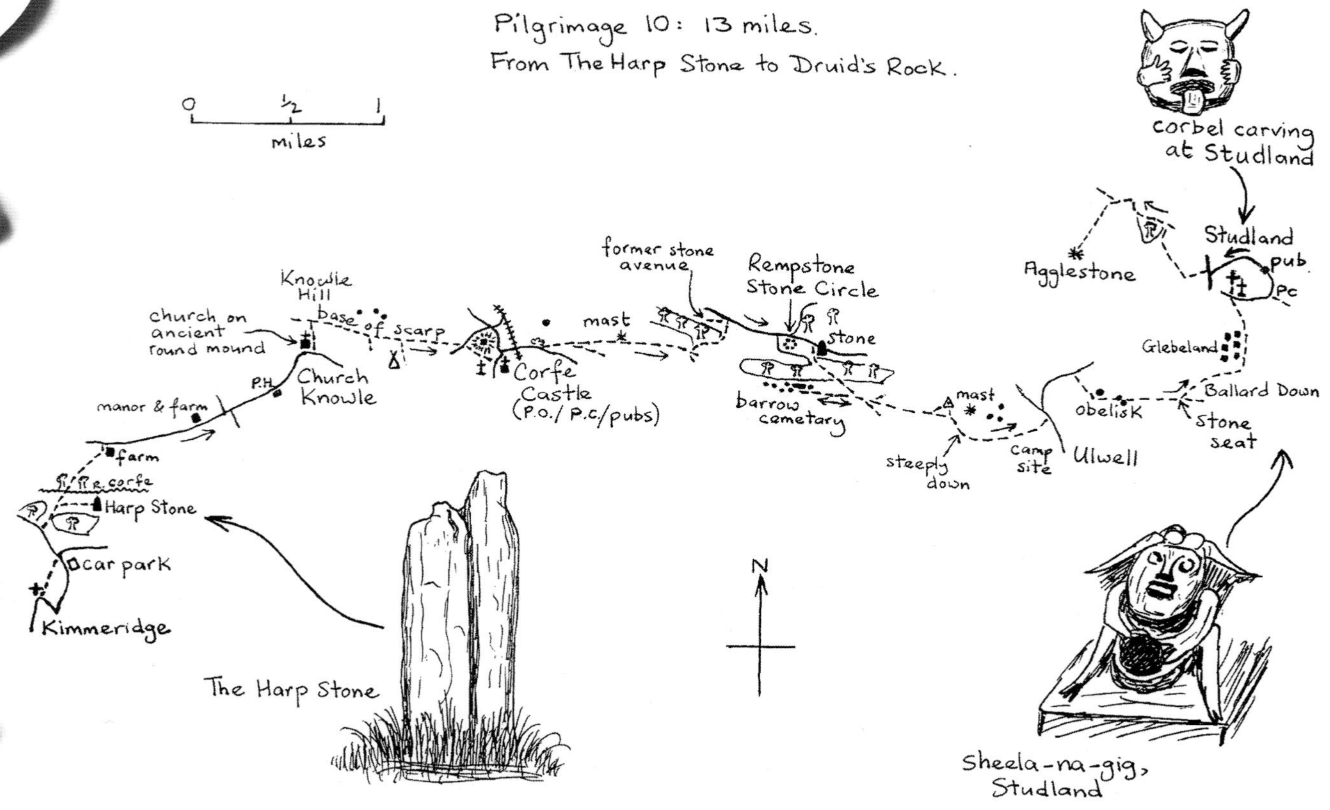

Pilgrimage 10: 13 miles.
From The Harp Stone to Druid's Rock.

0 ½ miles

corbel carving
at Studland

Studland
pub.
Pc

Ballard Down

Stone
seat

Glebeland

Agglestone

obelisk

Ulwell

Camp
site

N

mast

steeply
down

Rempstone
Stone Circle

stone

barrow
cemetary

former stone
avenue

mast

Corfe
Castle
(P.o./P.c/pubs)

base of scarp

Knowlie
Hill

Church
Knowle

church on
ancient
round mound

P.H.

manor & farm

farm

Little corfe

Harp Stone

car park

Kimmeridge

The Harp Stone

Sheela-na-gig,
Studland

PILGRIMAGE TEN

FROM HARP STONE TO
DRUID'S ROCK

A very scenic and enjoyable pilgrimage in the beautiful Purbeck Hills. Whilst walking is generally good underfoot some sections are quite steep and a little demanding. There is an all day café at Kimmeridge, a pub at Church Knowle plus an excellent choice at Corfe Castle including The Fox, said to be the oldest in Dorset. The Bankes Arms at Studland has a lovely scenic garden and open all day in summer.

Start from the car park at Kimmeridge.

OS Maps: Landranger 195 and Outdoor Leisure 15. Reference: 918/799.

Approximate distance: 13 miles. Rempstone Stone Circle is ideal for a split walk

L eave the car park turning right, go up beside the church of St Nicholas, out through the kissing gate and then climb the field making for the gap and stile at the top, go over into the lane and turn left. Upon reaching the bend cross the stile and bear right down to the gap in the corner of the field, cross the stile into the adjoining field and bear left down to the stile in the bottom hedge. To visit the Harp Stone divert right across the field. It is just visible from this path in the far hedge.

The Harp Stone near Kimmeridge, a prehistoric megalith.

127

The Harp Stone is the tallest remaining megalith in the Purbeck area. This 7 feet high prehistoric sentinel stands just south of the Corfe River on a gentle slope. Sacred sites in the vicinity of rivers are numerous in Dorset, good examples being the Nine Stones and the Muckleford Stone (both pilgrimage 4). The waters provided not only refreshment, but water for ritual. A close connection is known to exist also between water, standing stones and earth energies. Although the Harp Stone exhibits obvious phallic symbolism, on the east side of the stone there is a large hole (see SD plate 72), symbolic of the vulva of the Earth Mother, with a votive offering ledge beneath. In the hedgerow behind the stone lies a causeway down to the river, no doubt used for ceremonial purposes.

Rejoin the little path down through the copse, across the bridge, over the stile into the field and bear half right up and over the rise to the stiles. Bearing left cross the field to the stile then go up to the stiles in the corner turning left onto the farm driveway finally turning right in to the road.

Stroll along this peaceful lane for about a mile, a good spot to pick blackberries and sloes, until you reach Church Knowle. The New Inn provides a good refreshment stop before proceeding through the village to St Peter's church.

The church stands on a large round mound, a clear indicator of the Christianisation of a former sacred site. Churches at Toller Porcorum (Pilgrimage 1) and Whitchampton (Pilgrimage 9) were set

The old lime kiln, between Church Knowle and Corfe.

The approach to Corfe Castle, with the spine of the Purbecks beyond.

Corfe Castle, from the church.

up on very similar mounds. The church itself has a 13th century fabric, with modifications of c.1840. The plan is cruciform and inside is a fine 16th century canopied table tomb.

Take the signposted path on the right, leading to the gate, grass track and stile beyond. Turn right onto Knowle Hill. Further on there is an optional path on the left which although means a strenuous climb the views are better otherwise keep to the path ahead negotiating the occasional stile and gate. After passing the old lime kiln look out for Dartford warblers on the high gorse bank. Leave by the gate and bear left along the gravel path then turn right over the bridge, cross the road and join the path beneath the castle leading to the village centre. Corfe is well served with pubs and tea-rooms. The Fox Inn dating back to 1568 is reputed to be the oldest in Dorset and well worth a visit.

The Fox Inn, Corfe.

Much has been written on the interesting history of the castle and village. As we are partaking of pilgrimage we will focus on the spiritual aspects of the locality. The hill on which the castle ruins stand would certainly have been held sacred by our prehistoric ancestors. From the certain directions the hill takes on the form of a tummy or breast of the Earth Goddess. The hill in fact lies on a ley line linking it with several ancient sites in the Purbeck area, including the stone circle at Rempstone, to be visited later (see AS fig. 65 for ley map). In the centre of the village stands the cross, where every May Day local Morris dancers still gather, echoing ancestral Beltaine celebrations. The base and steps of the cross are medieval surmounted by a shaft and cross dating to 1897. Close by is the parish church of St Edward, dedicated to the 'King and Martyr' associated with folklore of miracles described in Chapter 2. The saint himself stands at the east end of the church roof. Look out too for the gargoyles up the tower and the carved heads on exterior stonework. Inside, the architecture is notable for numerous finely carved floral and foliated stonework. The church was largely renovated in Victorian times but earlier work, some 700 years old, can still be found (guide book available).

From the church head north down the main road soon to turn right into Sandy Hill Lane. Go under the railway line and straight ahead, ignoring the path on the left walking until you reach the gate on the left accessing the Purbeck Way signposted, to the Coast Path 5½. Further ahead bear left up to the ridge path, forking left through the gate by the radio mast and upward through another gate. Take time to look around and enjoy the magnificent panoramic views especially over Poole Harbour. Continue ahead gently climbing Brenscombe Hill but before reaching the stone marker on the left, branch off to the left and join the steep path which heads north down between the gorse bushes widening to a gravel track before reaching a gate. Keep to this attractive sunken track which drops steadily to the road.

Turn right and after passing Rempstone House the road climbs gently past a wood on the right wherein lies the Rempstone Stone Circle: (look for gaps in hedgerow).

This Bronze Age circle is in fact the focus of a cluster of stones and barrows, all interconnected and all with a spiritual emphasis (see AS figs 61 – 65 for ley, detailed maps and plans). An avenue of stones formerly stood west of the circle and some outlying megaliths have also been discovered. At the circle itself is a northern arc of ten stones that can usually be found amongst the trees, the southern part of the circle having been removed. The circle would have been around 85 feet in diameter with as many as 20 stones. The stones are deep red local Bagshot sandstone and interesting symbolism is hidden in some of them. As one enters the circle through the gap in the hedgerow walk around to the other side of the stone in front of you. A deep cavity is present half way up the stone. This would have been used for votive offerings and is symbolic of the vulva of the Earth Mother (see photograph). Working one's way east, clockwise, around the circle the third stone is of great interest. Peter Knight perceived head-like features some 4 years ago, making it the earliest discovered stone head in Dorset. Recent work by Terence Meaden at Avebury and elsewhere has shown that symbolic stone heads such as this are in

One of the Rempstone megaliths, a white flower marking the votive cavity.

below: The stone head, in right-facing profile, at Rempstone.

fact numerous and 8 are currently known in Dorset (see Dorset Earth Mysteries Group Journal No 1 for illustrated article by Peter Knight). The head at Rempstone has eyes, nose and mouth on BOTH SIDES, with hints of eyebrows, lips and nostrils too. The head faces the centre of the circle and would perhaps have represented deity during prehistoric rituals here. (see Pilgrimage 1,3 and 4 for other examples).

❖❖❖❖❖❖❖❖❖❖❖❖❖❖❖❖❖❖❖❖❖❖❖❖

I came across some fairy stones
In a dark wood one day.
I stood midst overgrown mysteries,
Sharing Earth and sky with tree and fern.
I smelt damp earth and decaying leaves
As lichen and moss competed for ancient crevices.
The dappled light traced dancing images,
A face here, an eye there, my imagination set free.
Ancient sentinels rising from the earth like dragons,
Holding court as I paid homage.
'Rempstone' by Peter Knight

❖❖❖❖❖❖❖❖❖❖❖❖❖❖❖❖❖❖❖❖❖❖❖❖

Continue east along the road until you reach the bridleway on the right signposted to Nine Barrow Down. A large stone is soon encountered to the left of the track.

The stone by the bridle track, east of Rempstone Stone Circle.

This large, prone stone is an outlier of the stone circle and may be from a former avenue of stones or, more likely, mark the ascent of a ceremonial track up to Nine Barrow Down, significantly just ½ mile south of the circle. The stone appears pointed at one end, possibly by human endeavour.

Keep to the main track, which rises fairly steeply through Kings Wood, an area of mixed woodland, before reaching a gate and the ridge beyond. This is Nine Barrow Down and we will take the ridge path west for a short distance to visit the barrows that give the down its name.

The setting for this major Bronze Age Barrow cemetery is breathtaking, with distant views north and south as well as along the spine of the Purbeck hills. The locality was chosen with great care by our ancestors so that the barrows could be seen from surrounding villages as well as the Rempstone Stone Circle below (now obscured by trees). 17 tumuli cluster around a single elongated long barrow, of Neolithic Age, indicating that this was a sacred place over many generations. The circle and the long barrow were focal monuments, clearly shown by the absence of barrows along the ridge for quite a distance. Some of the barrows have ditches and several of them form a line some 250 yards long, whilst the long barrow lies with other tumuli on slightly lower ground. This is one of the largest barrow groups in Dorset, rivalling those of the Ridgeway and Knowlton. After the steep ascent to the ridge it is an uplifting resting place, amongst ancestral chieftains and priests.

Plan of the barrow cemetery on Nine Barrow Down, dating c.3,300-c.1,700 BC. The long barrow aligns with equinox sunrises and sunsets.

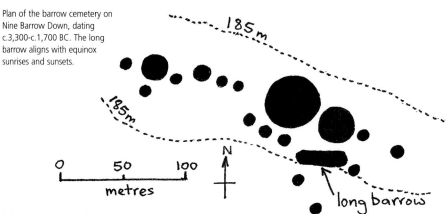

below: The cross at Studland.

Retrace your steps eastwards along the ridge path keeping straight ahead towards the small gate on the right, pass through then go through the gate on the left and continue ahead along the ridge through a couple more gates. As you approach the road bear left across the grass by the telegraph pole to the far gate which exits on the road junction.

Fork right up the hill, shortly crossing over to the safety of the grass verge on the left. Continue up and round the bend then cross to the bridleway and make your way up Ballard Down, through the gates, and past the obelisk following the ridge ahead until you reach the fingerpost beside the large stone seat. Fork left at this spot down the hillside picking up the grass and gravel track which drops down to meet a tarred lane eventually delivering you to the stone cross at Studland

The round base of the cross is Saxon whilst the remainder was erected in 1976, replacing a former shaft and cross head. The cross is an interesting blend of modern and ancient images, the craftsmanship of local mason Trevor Heysom. On the south side of the shaft are runes spelling out the inscription 'I created this world and I sustain this world' (see SD plate 20). On the underside of the cross head look for the symbols of the sun and the moon, representing Divine balance, female and male, yin and yang (see SD plate 67).

Proceed north along the lane, a short walk to the church.

The church of St Nicholas is the most complete Norman church surviving in Dorset, with some pre-Conquest stonework still visible as an added bonus. These earlier walls occur at the tower, whilst the remaining nave is 11 - 12 century. The porch is 17th century and an overall restoration took place in1880. Of particular interest are the 23 11th century corbel carvings, where the roof joins the walls on the outside. Ancient symbolism is displayed in many of them such as horned creatures, monkeys, a saltier (a broad diagonal cross with Celtic origins), tongue-pullers and, most rarely in Dorset, 2 Shella-na-gigs (another can be seen at Leigh, on Pilgrimage 2). Also on the outside of Studland church is a fine 8-petalled flower in stone at the NE corner, and in the porch some fine 12th century stonework. Inside, the chalice-shaped font is also 12th century.

Return to the cross, turning left following the lane down, round and up to the Bankes Arms, an excellent refreshment stop. Studland church.

The Agglestone, from the south.

Carry on past the pub, bearing left at the junction then right in to the road and in a few paces go up the little track on the left beside Stud Holme, footpath signed. Follow the path up to the stile, cross the field to the stile on the far side turning right onto the bridleway track. Walk for a while until you reach a wide gravel track then turn left, go past all the dwellings, through the gate, cross the bridge and turn left. Either stay on the sandy track which eventually reaches the Agglestone or divert left onto a signposted footpath, a shorter route but a little uneven with some steep steps.

People who visit the Agglestone for the first time are invariably taken aback by its sheer size. This huge natural outcrop of ironshot sandstone rises out of the heathland, perched on a small knoll. It is some 80 feet in circumference and weighs around 400 tons. The name probably derived from the Saxon 'halig' meaning 'holy' and rocks such as this would have been regarded as sacred by our distant ancestors. It has druid associations and folklore says the Devil threw the rock from the Isle of Wight, his target being either Corfe Castle or Bindon Abbey. Incredibly, the Agglestone does lie on a direct line between Corfe Castle and the Needles. Folklore concerning giants or the Devil slinging stones has been associated with ley lines (see AS page 166). The rock is also known as the 'Devil's Anvil' and 'Devil's Nightcap', hints perhaps of pre-Christian gatherings, which the church would have deemed unholy. The stone was formerly a loganstone, that it was capable of being rocked, and such stones have long been

above:
The Agglestone from the north. The huge face is shown, illuminated by the summer sun shinning obliquely from the east (left). The features are best appreciated from a distance. (see also SD Plate 81).

left: Looking north from the Agglestone across the heathland.

137

regarded as wishing stones. The Agglestone is an excellent locality to practise dowsing, its huge bulk and quartz-rich matrix attracting earth energies across the heath. Nearby is the Puckstone (AS page 75-77) and the surrounding land has numerous barrows, indicating that prehistoric Man held the area with some reverence. In 1998 Peter Knight became the first recorded person to note the large facial features on the north side of the rock. Eyes, nose, nostrils and gapping mouth survey the heath. Because of their size, the features are best perceived from some distance away, off the knoll itself. Across the world natural rock formations resembling heads and faces have been regarded as sacred places, many for thousands of years. As we stand below this 'Spirit of the Rock', to use an aboriginal term, we can ponder the pilgrimage, and perhaps, like the gigantic features above us, look into the new millennium with our eyes wide open, to experience the wonder and sanctity of this magical land.

❖❖❖❖❖❖❖❖❖❖❖❖❖❖❖❖❖❖❖❖❖❖❖❖❖❖❖❖

Agglestone, Halig Stone,
Sacred healing rock,
In footsteps of Druids am I,
'neath your mighty form,
You survey the open heath,
Your land, your domain,
With craggy skin and deep wild eyes,
Timeless face stares through the doorway of time,
Mouth open, speaking truths,
What is it you say to me?
As I dream, emersed by enfolding shadow,
Nurtured by ancient rock and crystal,
The wind caressing and cleansing my soul.
Agglestone, Hallowed Stone, here before men,
An eternity of moons you patiently waited,
For us to know you, Spirit of the Rock.
'Druid Rock', by Peter Knight.

❖❖❖❖❖❖❖❖❖❖❖❖❖❖❖❖❖❖❖❖❖❖❖❖❖❖❖❖

FURTHER INFORMATION

The following individuals and organisations can be contacted by those wishing to partake organised day trips or individual long distance pilgrimages, or else attend local visits to sacred sites.

PETER KNIGHT organises day trips to sacred sites across Dorset and Wiltshire. Write to him at 14 Maxwell Road, Winton, Bournemouth BH9 1DJ.

Dorset Earth Mysteries Group holds regular field trips and meetings on the subject of ancient sacred sites. Contact Peter Knight at the above address.

West of England Pilgrimage Association, 37 Devonshire Building, Bath BA2 4SU.

Vision Quest, PO Box 603, Bath BA1 2ZU,
(organises long-distance pilgrimages)

Source – The Holy Wells Journal, Pen-y-Bont, Bont Newydd, St Asaph, Dengighshire, LL17 0HH, Wales.

Pilgrim's Herald (journal of earth energies and sacred sites), The Rosses, Henbrook Lane, Brailes, Banbury, Oxon, OX15 5BA.

The Sacred Land Project (organised walks & the clearing of old pilgrimage routes). Manchester University, 799 Wilmslow Road, Manchester, M20 2RR

FURTHER READING

Adair J. The Pilgrim's Way, Saints and Shrines in Britain and Ireland. BCA London, 1978.

Bunyan, John. The Pilgrim's Progress, Penguin edition, 1965.

Castleden, Rodney. The Cerne Giant, Dorset Publishing Co. 1996

Cooke, Grace and Ivan. The Light in Britain, White Eagle Publishing, 1971

Devereux, Paul. Symbolic Landscapes, Gothic Image,1992

Devereux, Paul. Re-visioning the Earth, Simon and Schuster, 1996

Devereux, Paul and Thompson, Ian. The Old Straight Tracks of Wessex, Thorsons, 1992.

Dorset Earth Mysteries group, Journal No 1 1999.

Dorset Historic Churches Trust. A Choice of Dorset Churches, Friary Press. 1986.

Friar, Stephen. A Companion to the English Parish Church, Bramley, 1996.

Gant, Roland. Dorset Villages, Robert Hale, 1980.

Graves, Tom. Needles of Stone Revisited, Gothic Image, 1986.

Harte, Jeremy. Cuckoo Pounds and Singing Barrows, Dorchester. 1986.

Harte, Jeremy. Legends (Discover Dorset Series), Dovecote Press, 1998.

Heselton, Phillips. Secret Places of the Goddess, Capall Bann, 1995.

Hutchings, Monica. Hardy's River, Abbey Press, 1967.

Jones, S and Traskey, P. Milton Abbey, English Life Publications, 1997.

Kamar, Satish. No Destination, Green Books, Bideford, 1992.

Knight, Peter. Sacred Dorset-On the Path of the Dragon, Capall Bann, 1998.

Knight, Peter. Ancient Stones of Dorset, Power Publications, 1996.

Knight, Peter. Letters to the Wild Man -An Anthology, self-published, 2000.

McLuhan, TC. Cathedrals of the Spirit, Thorsons, 1996.

Meaden, Terence. The Secrets of the Avebury Stones, Souvenir Press, 1999.

Miller, H and Broadhurst, P. The Sun and the Serpent, Pendragon Press, 1989.

Morinis, Alan. Sacred Journeys: The Anthology of Pilgrimage, Greenwoods, 1993.

Murphet, Howard. Where the Road Ends, Macmillan, 1883.

Osborne, George. Exploring Ancient Dorset, Dorset Publishing Co., 1985.

Palmer, M & Palmer, N, Sacred Britain, Piatkus, 1997.

Peck, M Scott. In Search of Stones, Simon and Schuster, 1996.

Pennick, Nigel. Celtic Sacred Landscapes, Thames and Hudson, 1996.

Pope, Alfred. Old Stone Crosses of Dorset, Chiswick, 1906.

Power, Mike. Pub Walks in Dorset, Power Publications, 1997

Power, Mike. 40 More Pub Walks in Dorset, Power Publications 1998.

Power, Mike. and Flint, Brenda, Pub Walks in Hardy's Wessex, Power Publications, 1997.

Power, Mike. The Dorset Coast Path, Power Publications, 1990.

Power, Mike. Mike Power's Pub Walks along the Dorset Coast

Royal Commission on Historical Monuments. Inventory of Historical Monuments of Dorset, HM Stat. Office, 159-75.

Russell, George W. The Candle of Vision, University Books, New York 1965.

Sullivan, Danny. Ley Lines, Piatkus, 1999.

Sumpton, Jonathon. Pilgrimages: An Image of Medieval Religion, Faber and Faber, 1975.

Watkins, Alfred. The Old Straight Track, Abacus editon, 1974

Westwood, Jennifer. Sacred Journeys-Paths For the New Pilgrim, Gaia Books, 1997

Whitle, Jane. Twenty Wessex Walks Exploring Prehistoric paths, Hobnob, 1988.

INDEX OF PLACE NAMES

Toller Porcorum